The Girls' Guide to the SAT

Tips and Techniques for Closing the Gender Gap

The Girls' Guide to the SAT

Tips and Techniques for Closing the Gender Gap

By Alexandra Freer

Random House, Inc.
New York

www.PrincetonReview.com

The Independent Education Consultants Association recognizes The Princeton Review as a valuable resource for high school and college students applying to college and graduate school.

Princeton Review Publishing, L.L.C.
2315 Broadway
New York, NY 10024
Email: booksupport@review.com

ISBN 0-375-76240-X

Editor: Jeff Soloway

Director of Editorial Production: Maria Dente

Production Coordinator: Jennifer Arias

Manufactured in the United States of America.

9 8 7 6 5 4 3 2 1

ACKNOWLEDGMENTS

My sincere thanks to the many who helped me create this book: Victoria Printz, Sarah Kruchko, Allison Amend, Jenny Rikoski, Mindy Myers, Jennifer Nase, and Chris Vakulchik. In addition, I want to thank the many girls and boys who shared their thoughts, feelings and experiences with me by completing my questionnaire and/or meeting with me, especially the girls of Point Pleasant Borough High School and the PPPC Youth Connection. Thanks to Tom Russell, Jeff Rubenstein, Stephen White, Jennifer Arias, Marina Padakis, Maria Dente, Sarah Brockett, Tony Moore, and Jeff Soloway. Special thanks to Jeanne Krier of Random House for her support and her wonderful files. Also special thanks to my sounding-board, my pseudo-editor, and my dear friend Gabrielle Maisels—I could not have done this without you. This book would also not have been possible without the wonderful young women who cared for my sons: Rachel Zerbe and Lacey, Courtney, and Kelsey Norton, plus pinch-hitters Allison Tranter and "Aunt Vicky" Gianakos (and Mom for "buying" extra babysitters). Thanks to Harry and Maxi for keeping me company, and to my "moms" for always being there to lend support and encouragement. Finally, love and thanks to my husband Rob and my sons Jacob and Stephen, the most patient little boys I know.

CONTENTS

FOREWORD

While bookstore shelves are filled with SAT prep books, this is the only book you will find that is written for you. If you are a girl about to take the SAT, you must take this book seriously. Approximately 54 percent of the 1.2 million students who take the SAT each year are girls. While girls' GPAs in both high school and college are higher than their male counterparts, girls score approximately 40 points lower on the SAT than boys and have done so for decades.

40 points may not seem like a big deal. However, as you will see, those 40 points can keep girls from getting into colleges and participating in honors programs for which they are qualified. Those 40 points can also rob girls of the personal satisfaction and academic prestige of achieving high SAT scores.

For some girls, those 40 points are critical to their college experience. Female student-athletes, for example, must attain a minimum SAT score in order to be granted full playing eligibility. In 1994, 70 percent of female student athletes failed to achieve full-qualifier status because of their SAT scores.

40 points is also costing girls millions of dollars in scholarships and financial aid. Many colleges use "the numbers" to determine the appropriate financial aid package for each student. At some colleges, tuition scholarships are based solely on SAT scores. Even many independent scholarships consider the SAT a major factor in selecting recipients. For example, the PSAT (Preliminary SAT) is the sole qualifier for National Merit scholarships and recognition. Although approximately 56 percent of PSAT test takers are female, girls comprise only about 45 percent of National Merit Scholars.

Can a standardized test that is used as often and respected as highly as the SAT really be unfair to girls? In a word, yes. But proving this is no piece of cake. In the early 1980s, Phyliss Rosser, a feminist scholar, wrote a controversial article about the possible reasons for the gender gap. Energized by the controversy that ensued, she continued her research and ultimately wrote a book on the subject. In 1989, Kathleen Benjamin used Rosser's work to write the Young Woman's Guide to the SAT. While Benjamin's book has been out of print for some time, the gender gap remains with us today.

Girls' Guide to the SAT takes a refreshing approach to bridging the SAT gender gap. In it, we discuss seven main issues that contribute to girls' under-performance on the SAT. This is followed by practical, hands-on solutions for each area, providing powerful techniques and useful tricks designed to help each girl score her personal best on the test.

As you read Girls' Guide to the SAT, you'll feel both enraged and empowered: enraged by that fact that the test writers have knowingly perpetuated this inequity for decades, and empowered by the simple, effective strategies laid out for you. While your SAT score is not a measure of your intelligence or self-worth, it is your ticket to the college of your dreams. Read this book, practice the techniques and strategies, and do your part to close the gender gap once and for all.

Nancy Amanda Redd
A.B., Women's Studies, Harvard University, 2003
www.nancyredd.com

PART I
INTRODUCTION

INTRODUCTION

My first SAT score was a 1050. My second SAT score was a 1050. Now, a 1050 is not a bad score; however, a 1050 is not the score you should get when you're a track-one honors student graduating second in a class of 259 students. It's not a score that reflects your academic ability when you go on to graduate summa cum laude from college. And it's not the score that a straight-A student should get when fellow male classmates with much lower grades score in the 1400s.

I had always been a good test taker, taking the battery of standardized exams administered throughout school without concern, and typically scoring in the 95th percentile. In fact, I knew little about the SAT and went into the test assuming it would be much like those other standardized exams. I remember becoming more and more anxious during the test because I couldn't seem to work fast enough, didn't know whether to guess or leave something blank, couldn't tell if a question was as easy or hard as it seemed, etc. I remember thinking, "I could do well on this test if someone would just tell me the rules."

Well, as I said, a 1050 is not a bad score, but it's not a great score, and it was not a high enough score for me to get the kind of scholarship money I needed to attend the college of my dreams. Since my father was a professor at a small, private college (which meant I could go there tuition-free), I had no choice but to attend his school. My grades throughout college once again reflected my academic ability, and I was able to forget all about my embarrassing SAT score. Or so I thought.

During my junior year of college, I heard about an SAT test-prep company that was hiring. They wanted dynamic teachers and held an audition-style interview in which each applicant had to teach to a small group to demonstrate his or her teaching ability. I loved to perform and to teach and knew I could handle the subject matter once I was trained. I showed up prepared to dazzle the interviewers with my teaching ability, but was greeted first with a test—a Math and Verbal test composed of 40 difficult SAT problems to be completed in 30 minutes. I panicked. That old SAT 1050 was back to haunt me.

Luckily, the coordinator ran the teaching part of the interview before he checked the tests. He loved my teaching and hired me on the spot. A few days later, however, he called to warn me—I could attend the training, he said, but would have to work *really hard* to prove that I could teach the material, because my "test score was a little low." I was incensed, and determined to prove that I could handle the material.

I attended the teacher training course for The Princeton Review—an intensive program designed to ensure that every Princeton Review teacher knows everything there is to know about the SAT. After only one day of training, I was amazed at what I had learned. The training answered all those questions I had had when I sat in my high school cafeteria four years before. At the end of the training, we were required to take another full-length SAT under test conditions. This time I scored a 1450. Did I go up 400 points because of what

I had learned in college? Unlikely, since most of the material on the SAT is eighth and ninth grade-level stuff, and only weeks before I clearly didn't know enough of it to do well on a short quiz. Did I improve because I was less nervous during the test? Probably not, since this time I was taking the test to prove to my possible employers that I was bright and capable. If anything, I felt more pressure to do well than I did in high school.

The reason my scores improved so much in such a short period of time was that I learned the SAT. I learned what was on the test and what the test writers were looking for. I learned how to solve an analogy and how to use the techniques that make SAT Math problems easier. I learned when to guess and how to pace myself appropriately.

For the first time, someone had explained to me the rules of the SAT.

My story is similar to the stories of many young women. Although today many more students prepare for the SAT than did when I took it, the SAT scores of females still lag behind those of males. In 2002, female test takers scored an average of 1002, while male test takers scored an average of 1041. This difference of about 40 points represents a persistent gender gap in SAT scores that has existed for decades.

Is 40 Points a Big Difference?

Yes and no. Yes, because many colleges and universities use "the numbers"—SAT score and high school grade point average—almost exclusively to decide whom to accept and whom to reject. Yes, because even schools that consider more than just the numbers typically use the numbers first as a means of weeding out applicants. Yes, because, while females are getting lower SAT scores, they are earning higher grades in high school and college. And no, because 40 points represents, in most cases, just five or six questions. In other words, the score difference we are talking about—the difference that is keeping thousands of girls per year out of schools for which they are otherwise qualified—is the result of girls missing about five or six more questions than boys. That's it.

How Can You Close the SAT Gender Gap?

One question at a time. Learning who writes the SAT and what they expect might result in one more correct answer. Learning how to identify wrong answer choices quickly might get you another. Determining your personal pacing strategy could get you two more questions right. And so on.

You can close the SAT gender gap simply by preparing for the test. Most females are very "school smart": we know what it takes to do well in an academic environment and we can gauge from class to class and year to year exactly how much work we need to do to achieve our goals. And we know that being prepared is the key to success in school, at work, and throughout life. Yet, the SAT has been presented to us as something we cannot prepare for. In fact, many girls perceive it as some form of intelligence test. Nothing could be further from the truth. The SAT is simply a measure of how well you take the SAT. Although it is not a test of general knowledge or memorized facts, you can most certainly prepare for it by learning exactly what it is and what is expected from you. In other words, by learning the rules of the SAT.

How to Use This Book

This book was developed specifically for you: It was written by a woman, filled with the thoughts and ideas of other intelligent, capable women, and designed for young women like you who are about to take the SAT. In addition to interviewing my SAT students, I also surveyed and interviewed students from a local high school. Throughout the book, you will find quotes from these interviews and surveys. I chose to include these quotes because I believe that what students like you think is as important as, if not more important than, what all the "experts" have to say.

The concepts and strategies included in this book were chosen because they are what most girls need to know in order to score their personal best on the SAT. This is not to say that boys would not benefit from the information taught in this book, nor do I wish to give the impression that I am picking on guys throughout the book. But since we are talking about a *gender* gap, it is necessary to occasionally compare some typical behaviors of girls to those of boys. However, if I say that "girls are good at this," I am not implying that all boys are bad at it. If your brother or male friends read this book, tell them not to take it personally—this book is not about them; it's about *you*.

To get the most out of this book, I suggest you first read the chapters about the gender gap so that you fully understand the issue. Next, you need to spend time determining where *you* stand with the SAT. Chapter 3, What You Say, contains questionnaires and worksheets designed to help you pinpoint your main issues with the SAT. Work through this chapter thoroughly before going on to Part II of the book.

Part II's intro will give you some guidelines for working through the second half of the book. Work through the chapters in Part II in the order that is best for you. Each chapter contains techniques and strategies designed to help you score your personal best on the SAT. The goal of this book is to help you determine your individual plan for scoring your personal best. Take from this book what works for you; leave the rest.

What Else Should I Be Doing?

This book focuses on issues that are unique to female testers—something you won't find in any other SAT prep book. Working through this book will start you down the road to being completely prepared for the test.

I do suggest some further preparation, however. At a minimum, you need to practice what you are learning in the book by working through full-length SATs. To do so, purchase *10 Real SATs* (available in bookstores or through the College Board) and/or order copies of recent exams from ETS. Practicing the strategies you learn on real tests is the best way for you to get a handle on what real SAT questions feel like.

You may also wish to purchase a copy of The Princeton Review's *Cracking the SAT*. *Cracking the SAT* will provide you with more detailed strategies for the test, plus additional practice material. It's available in bookstores.

Finally, you may find after working through this book that you really want to work with an instructor. The Princeton Review offers courses and private tutoring throughout the country and around the world. For more information on taking a Princeton Review course in your area, call 1-800-2Review.

Are you ready to close the SAT gender gap? Let's go!

A Final Note

This book is yours. Don't be afraid to write in it. Use a pen, pencil, crayon, highlighter, or whatever implement you prefer. Circle examples, highlight words, circle major points. Write your thoughts in the margins, and mark your solutions to problems clearly and proudly. Writing is a very focusing, empowering activity, so do lots of it.

Chapter 1

What Is the Gender Gap?

What Is the SAT Gender Gap?

You and a male classmate each have a high school GPA of 3.49. You score a 1002 on the SAT (the female average) and he scores a 1041 (the male average). You both apply to the same two colleges. The first school creates a "composite score" by multiplying your GPA by 1000 and then adding it to your SAT score. Therefore, your composite score is a 4492 and your male classmate's is a 4531. The minimum score an applicant must have before the school will read his or her application is 4500. Your application is rejected. Your male classmate's application is reviewed, and he is accepted.

You are both accepted to the second school to which you apply. You both enroll at this college and register for the same courses, including the same math class. At the end of your freshman year, your GPA is a 3.5 and his GPA is a 3.4. Furthermore, you both received the same grade in your math class, even though he scored 34 points higher on the Math portion of the SAT than you did.

This scenario represents, in a nutshell, the SAT gender gap. Female testers currently score, on average, 39 points lower than male testers on the SAT (based on 2002 numbers); 34 points lower in Math and 5 points lower in Verbal. In fact, females have scored approximately 40 points lower than males on the SAT for as long as they've been taking the test.

So What's the Problem?

The fact that females score lower than males on the SAT is not, by itself, the problem. The problem is that the SAT is not living up to its stated purpose. The College Board, the organization responsible for the SAT, states that "The SAT is designed to help predict your freshman grades in college" (*10 Real SATs* 2002, 2). But the truth is that *women earn higher grades throughout college than men with the same SAT scores.* In other words, the SAT is not accurately predicting how females will do in college. It's "underpredicting" female college grades and "overpredicting" male college grades.

One could argue that some college grades are inflated, as are some high school grades. While this may be true, it is irrelevant. The SAT's only purpose is to predict college grades. If there is a discrepancy between the SAT and the grades students are receiving in college, then the problem lies with the SAT.

WHY DOES UNDERPREDICTING FEMALE COLLEGE GPAS MATTER?

As we all know, college admissions officers base their decisions, at least partly, and often heavily, on SAT scores. According to researchers at the University of California at Berkeley, because of the 40-point difference in SAT scores, *nearly 13,000 women per year are unfairly denied admission to large public universities* (Leonard and Jiang, 393). Since females' SAT scores are lower, and since admissions officers often give the same weight to SAT scores as to high school GPAs, many women are not even considered for admission by some schools, though they would likely do as well or better than male applicants with the same or higher SAT scores. Nearly half of the colleges and universities in the country base their admissions decisions solely on "the numbers" (standardized test scores and GPAs). And many schools that don't exclusively use SAT scores and GPAs to make admissions decisions typically *do* use the numbers as a means of initially weeding out applicants.

In the scenario discussed at the beginning of this chapter, you were rejected from consideration by the first university to which you applied based strictly on your numbers, while your male classmate was considered for admission and ultimately accepted. However, if you and your male classmate were to attend the same university and take the same courses, you would be likely to have a higher GPA than he would. The fact that you were rejected from consideration based on your numbers was unfair, because these numbers do not accurately represent how you would probably perform at the school.

> "[What] ETS calls a 'small underprediction' has significant consequences."
>
> (Leonard and Jiang, 393)

IT GETS WORSE

A 40-point average difference is small but significant. However, the difference between male and female scores on the high end of the SAT score range is even greater, and when you're competing for scholarship money or for those few spots at the most competitive colleges, differences at the high end of the score range are *very* significant.

According to the College Board's 2001 score report, of the 587 students who scored a 1600 on the SAT, 400 were male and 187 were female—a ratio of more than 2 to 1, male to female. Of the 1,979 students who scored 1500, 1,274 were male and 705 were female. At the score of 1400, the ratio of males to females was approximately 3 to 2.

At 1300, women still only made up about 44 percent of scorers. It is not until 1180 that males and females finally evened out.

What?

How can it be that this incredible discrepancy exists and no one is doing anything about it? To be fair, lots of people are trying to do something about it. More than 400 colleges and universities no longer require the SAT for admission. In fact, the entire California university system recently considered dropping the SAT from its admissions requirements—that's one of the reasons the SAT is going to be changed in 2005. However, the people with the power to make the biggest difference—namely the Educational Testing Service and the College Board—seem to be spending as much or more time defending the SAT as trying to improve it.

What's Going On?

Why are females scoring lower on the SAT, yet getting better grades in high school and college? Why do girls score substantially lower than boys on the Math portion of the SAT, even though they get better math grades in high school, and take and excel in similar math classes in college? And why on earth are girls scoring lower than boys on the Verbal SAT when in virtually all other verbal measures, girls significantly outperform boys?

Because Girls Don't Test Well, Right?

Some people think that males always do better than females on tests because females "just don't test well." On many other standard tests, however, females score just as well as males do. In 2001, the ACT—the other major test used by admissions officers to judge college applications—showed a score difference between males and females of only 0.2 points on a 36-point scale. No gender gaps were reported in Math or Science on the 2001 New York City Regents, although girls significantly outscored boys on Reading and Writing (Benfer, 2). And on the National Assessment of Educational Progress (NAEP), "girls of all ages, races, and ethnic backgrounds matched or surpassed boys' scores in reading and writing" (AAUW *Gender Gaps* 1998, 28). These are just a few examples of how girls are, in fact, "testing well."

What They Say

The SAT is put together by a company called the Educational Testing Service (ETS). ETS is a very big company located just outside Princeton, New Jersey. ETS has made a lot of money selling not only the SAT, but also about 500 other tests, such as tests for CIA agents, golf pros, travel agents, and barbers. The company that hires ETS to write the SAT is called the College Entrance Examination Board, or the College Board for short.

ETS and the College Board explain the SAT gender gap in several ways. (Yes, they do know about the gender gap and have known for a very long time.) First, the College Board states that the gender gap exists because more females than males take the test, and "in testing, as numbers go up, scores tend to go down" (College Board, "What Should You Know," 4) However, this trend doesn't hold true on many other tests. In fact, a study of several Advanced Placement exams (also written by ETS) showed exactly the opposite—on the tests in which males scored better than females, the gender gap was greatest when the male testers significantly outnumbered the female testers(Gipps and Murphy 1994, 245–246).

Not at the Top

"Twice as many males as females achieve SAT scores over 700. If the scoring gap were caused solely by the larger pool of females taking the exam, females should still attain the same percentage of high scores as males. In fact, the opposite is true: The gender gap is largest in the highest score ranges."

(FairTest, "Gender Bias," 4)

The College Board also claims that girls do not take as many rigorous mathematics and science courses in high school as boys (College Board, "What You Should Know," 4). However, according to numerous studies, this is simply not the case. Even if it were true, this explanation would only make sense if the Math section of the SAT tested rigorous high school Math, which it currently does not. In addition, girls' math scores have not increased relative to boy's in the last few decades, even though girls are taking more rigorous math courses than they were 30 years ago. Finally, different course-taking patterns in math and science certainly would not explain why females score lower on the Verbal portion of the SAT, especially since females tend to score higher on virtually all other tests of verbal ability.

As further explanation, the College Board states that female SAT takers come from families with lower incomes and have parents with less education (College Board, "What You Should Know," 4). I'm not sure what demographic sources they used to arrive at this conclusion, but in the same document the College Board states that "differences in scores persist despite similarities in family income and parental education…". (College Board, "What You Should Know," 2–3). Does this not imply that groups (such as girls) who currently score lower on the SAT would continue to do so even if their families became wealthy and well educated? How, then, does the socioeconomics of females explain the gender gap if the gap would exist anyway?

Finally, the College Board states that "male and female scores may also reflect different interests, learning styles, and strengths at various stages of development." (College Board, "What You Should Know," 4). Well, if the test is supposed to reflect students' strengths at various stages of development, why are females scoring lower on the Verbal section when studies indicate that the average 16-year-old boy has the reading skills of an average 14-year-old girl? (Benfer, 2) Furthermore, keep in mind that these "learning styles" are the same ones that are helping females attain higher grades in college.

Which brings us back to the main point: If the SAT is designed to predict grades and it is not predicting female grades accurately, then something is wrong with the SAT.

Wait Until 2005

ETS is currently working on giving the SAT a major face lift. The New SAT, which will be administered for the first time in March of 2005, will include a Writing section (with both multiple-choice questions and an essay) and more advanced math questions; it will not include Analogies or Quantitative Comparisons.

Why all the changes? A lot of universities have begun to question the value of the SAT as a predictor of student ability. In fact, as mentioned previously, the entire California university system was considering dropping the SAT from its admissions requirements. Will the new test be more fair to girls? The Writing section will help, but the other aspects of the SAT that disadvantage girls will remain an integral part of the test.

Do They Mean It?

Is the SAT actually biased against females? Does ETS intentionally write it to be that way? The question of whether a test is truly biased is difficult to answer. In some ways, the SAT is biased against females because if a girl and a boy of equal ability take the SAT, the girl is more likely to score lower than the boy. However, this is not to say that ETS is intentionally making the SAT biased against women. It's just that, well, the methods they are using to prevent this bias aren't working.

What's the DIF?

ETS tests out all SAT questions ahead of time by giving them to test takers in the form of an unscored "Experimental" section on each SAT. The results are then analyzed for gender bias, among other things. So, if ETS is checking questions for bias, why does the SAT still have a gender gap? Because the way they test for bias is flawed. ETS uses a method called Differential Item Functioning, or DIF. The purpose of DIF is to identify items on which individuals of "similar ability" but of different gender or ethnicity performed differently.

For example, if, on an experimental section, most boys got question 6 right and most girls of similar ability got it wrong, question 6 would most likely not be used on a real test. The same would hold true, of course, if most girls got question 8 right and most boys of similar ability got it wrong.

But...

This, in fact, is one of ETS's problems. How does ETS determine which students are of "similar ability"? It uses their SAT scores, of course. But females are already scoring lower than they should be. If ETS uses DIF to remove items that give females a score advantage on the SAT, then they are perpetuating the gender gap by removing items that might allow women to even out the scores.

What's Really Going On

First, let's clarify one thing: The SAT measures how well one takes the SAT. Period. Unfortunately, in the United States, doing well on the SAT translates into more and better choices of colleges and universities, greater access to scholarship money, and higher placement in first-year college classes. It is not the *test* that measures all of these things—it is simply the educational system's use of the test that gives the SAT its meaning and status. That said, it is still important and necessary to examine why girls are scoring lower than boys on the SAT and to correct this problem; the SAT still stands between you and the school you want to attend. If the explanations offered by the College Board and ETS do not adequately account for the difference in girls' and boys' scores on the SAT, then what does?

Some of the gender gap is a direct result of the way the test is written. It is also perpetuated by other factors, such as the way girls respond to certain aspects of the test because of how they have been socialized and educated. Chapter 2 will take an in-depth look at the seven main areas that are contributing to the gender gap. While all seven areas may not apply to you, understanding each of these areas will help you begin to see which of them are affecting your SAT performance. Knowing what causes the gender gap for you is your first step toward closing the gap.

YOU CLOSE THE GAP

Regardless of what you think of the SAT and of ETS's role in the gender gap, you still have to take the test. The SAT is not going to be dropped anytime soon from the admissions policies of most colleges and universities. Therefore, it is up to you to close the gender gap. You are a good student. You know how to study for an important test. You've chosen this book, which will give you the information and resources you need to score your personal best. If every girl were to prepare for the SAT by using her scholastic strengths combined with information specifically designed for female testers, the SAT gender gap would be a closed issue.

Chapter 2
The Causes of the Gender Gap

WHAT'S CAUSING THE GENDER GAP?

The factors causing the SAT gender gap can be broken down into seven main areas: overall test issues, specific math issues, specific verbal issues, time constraints, assertiveness and guessing, concentration, and nerves. This list may be daunting, but rest assured: This book provides a solution for each problem area. Let's take a sneak peek at each solution:

Solution #1: Know the Test—Uncertainty about who is testing you and what you're being tested on can affect anyone's test performance. Many girls feel that knowing the SAT—learning exactly what is expected and what the "rules" of the test are—is the most important thing they can do to improve their scores. Learn how the test is structured, who is testing you, and what the best way to approach each question is, and you will *know the test.*

Solution #2: Do the Math—Girls do better on certain types of math questions, while boys do better on others, and on this test, there are more for *them* then there are for *you.* Level the playing field by learning to *do the math*—SAT Math, that is.

Solution #3: Get Verbal—Females should be scoring as well as or better than males on the Verbal portion of the SAT, as they do on every other test of verbal ability. But the SAT Verbal section tests a very limited set of verbal skills. *Get verbal* by learning exactly how to solve each type of verbal question you encounter.

Solution #4: Take Your Time—There are two ways in which time constraints adversely affect female testers: (1) Time constraints force girls to work through problems *quickly* as opposed to *carefully,* and (2) The pressure induced by time constraints can break concentration and induce anxiety for some girls. Yet, many aspects of time pressure are an illusion. Learn how to *take your time* on the SAT and your timing trouble will dissipate—or disappear.

Solution #5: Work Smart, Guess Smart—The SAT does not reward careful consideration as much as aggressive guessing. On the SAT, the *shortest* route to the correct answer is the *best* route. And guessing well—as opposed to just guessing—will yield the highest return. Use your insider's knowledge to *work smart, guess smart,* and do well.

Solution #6: Concentrate—Many girls report feeling distracted during the SAT. Figure out what distracts you, prevent the distractions that are within your control, and then hone your concentration skills so that you can *concentrate* anywhere, anytime, and on any test.

Solution #7: Be a Little Nervous—Major tests make many people nervous, even when they're well prepared, but girls cite nerves and anxiety as hurting their performance more often than boys do. While a little nervous tension can be useful, a lot can be distracting. Learn the right balance for you, and then build a supply of anxiety reducers so you'll only *be a little nervous* on test day.

As you read through this chapter, you might find yourself thinking, "That's me, that's what I do" over and over again. On the other hand, you may feel that only some of these areas are relevant to you. While you read, note your reaction to each area (remember, you can write anywhere in this book—use your white space freely). When you get to Chapter 3, you will use these notes to help you determine which areas are most relevant to you.

Ready? Let's find out what bugs you (and most other girls) about the SAT.

What's Up with That Test?

You know, and I know, that we girls have a lot of school smarts. By this I mean that we understand what it takes to do well in various academic environments. We know, for example, that Ms. H's physics class will be a breeze as long as we finish all the labs, but that Ms. C's Shakespeare class will take a ton of homework time. We know that that upcoming trig exam won't be too tough, but we'd better study our butts off for that American history final. In other words, we do well in school not only because we know how to study, but also because we know *what* to study, and how much to study.

But I Didn't Think We Could...

Many people, encouraged by propaganda from ETS and the College Board, continue to believe that the SAT is a test for which you cannot really prepare. Students often view the SAT as some form of intelligence test. Now, ETS and the College Board at least acknowledge that becoming familiar with the test is helpful—they have to, since they now sell prep materials. But they denounce prep courses and the like, claiming that you cannot substantially increase your scores by studying. For many people, particularly girls, going into such an important test without studying makes them anxious from the get-go.

Amy, 17

"My parents wouldn't send me to a prep course. They said that I was a good student and had good grades, so they expected that I would do well on the SAT too. I didn't do as well as I could have, and I know it's because I felt so unprepared going into the test."

Rachel, 19

"I didn't study for the test because I didn't know what to study. Our English teacher gave us a list of vocabulary words to study, but I didn't see the point of reviewing 100 vocabulary words that may or may not be on the test. I felt so awkward walking into such an important test and knowing that I was underprepared."

YES, YOU CAN STUDY FOR THE SAT

Studying improves your test grades in school. Why would it be any different for the SAT? Developing your own personal test-taking strategy based on sound test-taking advice, plus practicing your techniques on actual SATs, will make a marked difference in your confidence and your scores. The first step in preparing for the SAT is learning who writes the test and what is expected of you, the test taker.

WHO ARE THEY AND WHAT DO THEY WANT?

Your history teacher, Ms. Applegate, likes details. How do you know this? Because she spends an inordinate amount of time covering every little detail of each era studied. Therefore, when it comes time for an essay test in Ms. Applegate's class, you know that your essay had better include painstaking descriptions of every aspect of the time period being covered. Ms. Berardi, on the other hand, is a no-nonsense, to-the-point social studies teacher. Should an essay written for Ms. Berardi include the amount of detail that an essay written for Ms. Applegate should? No way; not if you want a good grade. Females tend to figure this stuff out, while our male counterparts often don't quite get it (no offense, guys). Boys will more often than not write the same essay, regardless of who they are writing it for; girls are more likely to write an essay tailored to the instructor who will be reading it. In the long run, possessing the ability to write to differing audiences—and to anticipate what will appeal to different individuals—is an immense help in both college and the professional world.

On the SAT, knowing who's testing you is just as helpful. This is particularly true since the SAT is not testing you on the stuff you are learning in high school. You can't review facts and information you've learned in school; therefore, you must prepare for the SAT by learning how it's put together and what the test writers expect. Learning the SAT, then, is akin to understanding what goes into the making of the test and how to use that information to your advantage.

WHAT ARE THEY TESTING ANYWAY?

If the SAT is not testing what you are learning in school, then what is it testing? According to ETS, the SAT assesses your critical thinking skills and insight by evaluating your verbal and mathematical reasoning abilities. But this doesn't make sense. First of all, isn't testing verbal and math skills an awfully narrow means of assessing insight or critical thinking ability? And even if the SAT did successfully assess a student's verbal and mathematical reasoning abilities (which it doesn't), how could those results alone accurately predict a student's entire college potential?

Many of the girls I've taught have expressed their frustration with the fact that the SAT doesn't test what they know. One student I surveyed said, "I feel like the stuff that is tested on the SAT has nothing to do with what I am learning in school. How can it predict my academic ability?" Good point. After all, college is about content as much as high school is.

Now That I'm Here...

"I got a 4.0 this past year at college, and it had nothing to do with my SATs. The things I studied in high school gave me the knowledge I needed to do so well."

PREP DIFFERENTLY

So, how do you *study* for the SAT if it's not testing what you've learned in school? By learning to think like the SAT test writers. Chapter 4, Know the Test, will teach you who writes the test, how they write it, and what the rules are.

Solution #1: Know the Test will help you close the gender gap by

- ✓ teaching you how the test is structured and what this means to you as the test taker
- ✓ introducing you to who writes the test, how they do it, and what their expectations are
- ✓ showing you essential SAT techniques, such as Process Of Elimination

MATH PROBLEMS

The larger score gap between females and males is on the Math portion of the SAT. In 2002, females scored 34 points lower than males on the Math portion of the test. Yet numerous studies have shown that females do as well as or better than their male counterparts in high school and college math courses. In fact, an article that appeared in the *Chicago Sun-Times* on January 13, 2002, opened by saying: "Two researchers say they have found the answer to the long-standing question of why boys do better than girls in math: They don't." (Wilson, 1)

Our society has long believed that boys are better at math and girls are better at English. In fact, back in the early days of evolutionary theory, Charles Darwin was even able to "explain" from an evolutionary perspective exactly how it was that men were more intellectually capable than women in all areas, including mathematics. These alleged biological differences have been disproved, of course, as women have demonstrated an equivalence of skill across all subjects, including math.

No Math Problems Here

"...[Recent] studies indicate that girls have significantly bridged historical gender gaps in math and science scores (and in some studies, have eliminated them entirely) and have held on to their historical advantage over boys in reading and writing skills." (Benfer, 1)

SO WHAT IS CAUSING THE GAP IN MATH SCORES?

The SAT Math gap may be due, in part, to the composition of the SAT Math section itself. Several studies indicate that females excel on certain types of math questions while males excel on other types.

For example, it is stated in the book, *Gender and Fair Assessment*, that males significantly outperform females on geometry and word problems, while females perform significantly better than males do on "intermediate algebra and arithmetic and algebraic operations" (Willingham and Cole, 171). Other researchers concur, stating that girls tend to do well on math questions that involve computation, logic, and combined arithmetic and algebra skills, while boys tend to do best on word problems and questions involving combined arithmetic and geometry skills (Dean, 2).

Carol Dwyer, an ETS researcher, makes the point that the "proportion of each type of item included in a particular test would likely determine the degree of disparity between males' and females' scores." (Selkow, 25) A non-scientific look at the Sunday, May 2000 SAT in *10 Real SATs* shows that approximately thirty-three of the sixty math problems on the test are geometry or word problems. Could the cause of the math gender gap be as simple as a distribution of question types that ends up favoring males? It only takes about five or so questions to create a score difference of thirty-four points. ETS' own researchers know that males perform better on certain types of math questions and females perform better on other types of math questions. Should they not strive to include equal numbers of each of these types of questions? ETS argues that the content it selects for the test is "educationally important" and that if the content "is critical for college work, then that justifies the decision to include it, even if it leads to gender differences." (Cole, 22) Is being able to solve combined arithmetic and geometry skills more important to college work than being able to solve combined arithmetic and algebra skills? Interestingly, comparative grades in calculus imply that it is not. A study called "The ETS Gender Study" shows that the SAT underpredicts female college calculus grades. (Cole, 20).

SOLVE THIS INEQUALITY

One student I surveyed had straight As and A+s in track-one math courses, yet scored a 450 on the Math section the first time she took the SAT. She reported, "I feel the SAT does not accurately represent my academic ability because most of the math has nothing to do with high school math, only logical reasoning." This discrepancy between math grades and SAT scores was common among the girls surveyed. Many girls reported primarily A's with occasional B's in higher-level math classes, yet had SAT Math scores typically in the 500s. By contrast, several of the boys who attended the same school and took the same math classes reported Math scores in the 600s, though their grades in math classes were typically B's with some C's.

BUT IT'S MATH

The American Association of University Women (AAUW) released a study in 1991 that shook up the country. The study, *Shortchanging Girls, Shortchanging America,* was the first of its kind to link the significant loss of girls' self-esteem in early adolescence with what they learn in school. According to the study, as girls "learn" that they are not as good at math and science as boys (through various unconscious practices of many schools), their aspirations and sense of self-worth deteriorate. Throughout my years as an SAT teacher, far too many of my female SAT students have said, "I'm just not good at math." Now, some of you may not be good at math. And some of you may be good at math but not like it very much. And some of you may have the potential to be good at math, but somewhere along the line "learned" that you were not. Whatever the case may be, it is important that you understand that females are just as good at math as males—if *you* don't like math or feel that you're not good at math, it has nothing to do with the fact that you're female.

Meghan, 19

"600 is a decent score, but it did not accurately reflect my abilities in math. I had very high grades and in general was confident with my skills.... The time constraint made me very nervous and unable to answer thoroughly."

Math Solutions

Regardless of your math ability, you can learn SAT math. The current SAT Math section (until March 2005) covers concepts you learned primarily in middle school. Plus, a lot of SAT math problems can be solved without doing very much math. Chapter 5, Do the Math, will teach you *SAT math*—the only math you need to know to raise your SAT Math score.

Solution #2: Do the Math will help you close the gender gap by

- ✓ teaching you math techniques that will increase both your speed and your accuracy
- ✓ focusing on the types of questions that occur most often on the SAT
- ✓ building your SAT math skills and math confidence

Verbal

Although the score difference between girls and boys on the Verbal portion of the SAT is much smaller than the difference on Math, it is just as significant, because, as I've mentioned, on virtually all other tests of verbal ability females score higher than males. For example, on the 2001 Regents exam in New York City, 70 percent more girls than boys had exemplary scores in Reading and Writing, and 45 percent more boys than girls scored well below grade level (Benfer, 2). In recent years, many educators have become greatly concerned with the overall performance of *boys* in school, particularly in the areas of reading and writing. If girls tend to score *higher* than boys on most tests of verbal ability, why are girls scoring *lower* on the Verbal portion of the SAT? Because the current SAT Verbal section doesn't truly test verbal ability.

What Is Verbal Anyway?

When you hear someone say, "She has strong verbal skills," what do you picture? Someone who's articulate. Someone who's an engaging writer. Someone who's good at grammar. Someone who is a good communicator. Someone who can comprehend difficult reading material. These all are important verbal skills, skills in which girls tend to excel. Yet none of these verbal skills is tested by the SAT. What does the Verbal portion of the SAT test? Nearly half the SAT verbal questions primarily test vocabulary, and the other half of the questions—the critical reading questions—test your ability to find details quickly.

SAT-V Is for Vocabulary

Each of the 30-minute Verbal sections on the SAT begins with a set of fill-in-the-blank statements (a.k.a. "sentence completions"), followed by a set of analogies—*this word* is to *that word* as *this word* is to *that word*, etc. What verbal skill do these two types of questions assess? In a word, *vocabulary.* It's true that you need to be able to read and "comprehend" in order to do sentence completions. And you do need to be able to identify the relationship between two words in order to solve an analogy. But what you really need in order to do well on these two SAT question types is a strong SAT vocabulary. Now, many girls with strong verbal skills also have strong high school–level vocabularies. However, an *SAT vocabulary* and a high school vocabulary are not necessarily the same thing. SAT vocabulary ranges from reasonably challenging words to very difficult words to downright absurd words.

If ETS wanted to assess vocabulary, they could simply have included a Vocabulary section. But because the SAT vocabulary assessment is disguised as something more, it is sometimes tricky to see these questions for what they are. In addition, many testers don't know the "rules" for solving either of these types of questions. They therefore attempt to solve them in ways that are inefficient and bound to lead them into the traps that ETS has waiting.

But You Do Need to Read

And the other half of the questions? Ah, critical reading. There seem to be a few things going on with the critical reading passages that make them more challenging for girls. The first problem with SAT critical reading passages is that they are not really written to be read.

Don't Read Me

To create an SAT critical reading passage, test writers typically take an excerpt of writing from some literary source and then edit it to suit their purposes. Of course, the only purpose of an SAT critical reading passage is to provide answers to a number of questions. Therefore, when a test writer edits a passage, she edits out virtually all the "inessential" information from the passage—anything that doesn't either answer a question or make a good wrong answer. In other words, she removes most of the stuff that makes reading *reading*. What you're left with is a dense passage that's difficult to read because it's packed with facts that you may or may not need to know in order to answer a question.

Many of us tend to approach an SAT reading passage as we would any other piece of writing: We read carefully, paying attention to detail and attempting to gather all the salient points as we go. Unfortunately, because the passages on the SAT are so dense, our attention to important detail rapidly overwhelms us. This is because everything we read is an important detail. We find ourselves thinking, "Okay, this is important... and so is this, and this, and this...". As we realize the whole passage is important, we realize, too, that we cannot possibly remember enough detail to answer all the questions we are given, nor do we feel we have the time to go back and forth countless times between the questions and passage. The density of the passages, combined with the time constraint, then, becomes a serious challenge to us that we typically haven't experienced before.

What About Me?

Multiple researchers have also pointed out that SAT critical reading passages contain an abundance of references to males, particularly famous male figures, while the references to females are rather meager (Dean, 2; Selkow, 25–30). Many question whether this inequity really matters to girls. According to Carol Dwyer, former ETS researcher, "It is common knowledge among test makers that gender differences can be manipulated by simply selecting different test items" (FairTest, "Gender Bias," 3). And apparently, ETS did just that back in the 1970s. Girls did score higher than boys on the verbal section of the SAT before the 1970s. After several years of this "imbalance," ETS determined that the Verbal test needed to be "balanced" more in favor of males. To do this, they added more questions that were of a subject matter that tended to favor males. Since that time, males have outscored females on both the Math and Verbal sections of the test.

> "What most people do not realize, however, is that the Verbal portion of the test is also biased. It has been shown that men do best on reading passages which involve mostly men while women do best on questions involving either mostly women, or, equal numbers of both. The SAT is filled with passages featuring men while any mention of women is rare." (Dean, 2)

Verbal Solutions

Luckily, there are many ways you can take control of the Verbal section of the SAT. Once you learn how the Verbal section is constructed, you can use that structure to your advantage. In all likelihood, you already have strong reading and verbal abilities. Now you need to develop equally strong *SAT* verbal skills. Combine your verbal strengths with test know-how and watch your Verbal score climb!

Solution #3: Get Verbal will help you close the SAT gender gap by

- ✓ teaching you to solve sentence completions without trying to figure out which word "sounds good"
- ✓ helping you to see analogies as the vocabulary test that it is
- ✓ showing you how to "stash" SAT vocabulary words
- ✓ outlining a proven method for answering critical reading questions

So Much to Do, So Little Time

Tests can be timed in order to assess how quickly one can perform a task, or for purely administrative purposes, or for a little bit of both. The SAT falls into the last category—it is timed so schools can schedule proctors for the day and know when the test will be over and also, according to ETS, in order to assess which students are "more insightful" (Willingham and Cole, 199–200). How do timed tests measure insight? ETS believes that if you put a question on a test that can be solved either by a long way or by a shortcut, the more insightful student will use the shortcut. If you fill a test section with such problems, the more insightful student will score higher because the less insightful student will take longer to solve the questions and therefore will not complete as many. Using speed to measure insight is an interesting theory, but it seems to backfire when it comes to boys and girls and the SAT. Instead of assessing students' insight, the SAT ends up assessing students' willingness to be aggressive and take shortcuts. And girls are less likely than boys to take shortcuts.

It is also interesting that ETS would choose to predict freshman year grades by using a timed test. Accuracy, diligence, perseverance, and creativity are far more important attributes for success in college than the ability to solve a problem quickly. For example, my college physics final consisted of one problem: Construct a launch with a ramp that will propel a ball into a cup on the floor. If you completed all calculations properly, and the ball went into the cup on the first attempt (no trial runs), you got an A on the final. If it took two tries, you got a B. Three tries, a C, and so on. I didn't rush through that test.

And yes, I got an A—by considering every angle, meticulously working through each calculation, and double-checking my work. Requiring students to complete problems in one minute or less tests gamesmanship, not college ability. Some of the brightest individuals I know are downright slow when it comes to developing solutions to problems or expressing new ideas. It's not a bad thing to solve problems quickly. But speed does not directly relate to college success, and that's one of the problems with the SAT.

More Than a Matter of Time

In addition to the literal challenges caused by the time constraints of the SAT, girls also seem to respond more negatively to the very existence of time constraints on the test. Interestingly, many girls do not feel this same pressure on other timed exams. One student I spoke with said, "I never found those other standardized tests you take in school difficult to finish—I always finished early. That's why I was so thrown by the SAT." Virtually every girl I spoke with identified time pressure as the number one reason they felt they did not perform as well as they could have on the SAT. One student commented, "I knew I could do all the problems on the Math section, but some of them would require a lot of time. If I started to feel like I was working on one problem for too long, I would start worrying about the time and not be able to concentrate on finishing the problem." Becoming anxious, not being able to concentrate, and having trouble deciding how to solve a problem quickly are all feelings girls have expressed to me concerning SAT time constraints. Unfortunately, there is little chance that the SAT will ever become untimed. However, there are ways you can reduce or remove the time pressure from your SAT.

Timing Solutions

Solution #4: Take Your Time will help you reduce time pressure by helping you determine your most accurate, efficient pace. It will also show you how to gradually increase your testing speed without sacrificing accuracy. And it will provide you with a variety of timing drills to do during the weeks leading up to the test to help you find your SAT testing groove.

Solution #4: Take Your Time will help you close the gender gap by

- ✓ helping you determine which problems you need to do—and which you don't need to do—in order to attain the score you want
- ✓ teaching you to increase your SAT pace without sacrificing accuracy
- ✓ reducing the anxiety time pressure can cause by helping you find your SAT groove
- ✓ providing you with multiple timing drills for practice

Assertiveness and Guessing

As I mentioned, according to ETS, insightful testers will see the shortcut to a problem and take it; everyone else will end up doing the problem the long way. In addition, multiple-choice questions encourage testers to look for shortcuts by design. However, girls are often less likely than boys to take the shortcut. This may by one reason why studies have found that females tend to not do as well on multiple-choice questions as on any other type of question. Studies have found that females tend to excel on short answer, essay, and constructed response questions as compared to multiple-choice questions. And, as you know, other than the ten grid-in questions in Math, the SAT is all multiple-choice.

> "Of course standardized tests are biased. But it is not just standardized tests—any single testing method is biased because it applies just one approach to getting at student knowledge and achievement. Any single testing method has its own particular set of blinders. Since the bias in testing is intrinsic in the form of assessment used, we cannot eliminate this problem simply by changing the question asked. Rather, we must ask the question in many different ways."
>
> —Jonathan Suporitz, author of "From Multiple Choice to Multiple Choices." (AAUW *Gender Gaps,* 40–41)

Where's My Answer?

Multiple-choice questions also leave little room for creative thought. To get a multiple-choice question right, you must be able to identify the correct answer as someone else perceives it. How often on a critical reading passage have you come up with an answer in your head, only to read all the choices and realize that you perceived the question differently from how the test writer intended? If you were writing an essay or constructing your own response, you could explain your logic. On a multiple-choice test, you have no option but to align your thinking with that of the test writer.

In some ways, females should have an advantage over males in this area. After all, we are the ones with the knack for tailoring our responses to our readership. Therefore, once you know what the SAT test writers expect, multiple-choice questions will become easier for you. However, the timed multiple-choice format of the SAT is a challenge to girls for another reason—it strongly rewards aggressive guessing.

Pick a Letter, Any Letter

Aggressive guessing can improve a test taker's score by increasing both her speed and her correct answers from *educated* guesses. However, studies have shown, and the girls I have spoken with agree, that females tend to shy away from guessing when they don't know an answer (FairTest, "Gender Bias" 3–4). Just as avoiding shortcuts will hurt your score, being unwilling to guess on the SAT will also keep you from achieving your best score.

Kate, 18

"I couldn't bring myself to answer a question if I only sort of knew the answer. I knew that that was what I was supposed to do, but I just kept thinking, 'I should know this, I should know this…'"

Work Smart, Guess Smart

Solution #5: Work Smart, Guess Smart will help you understand what it means to work smart and guess smart and why it's important for you to do so. It will also give you drills so you can practice and hone your skills.

Solution #5: Work Smart, Guess Smart will help you close the gender gap by

- ✓ helping you put yourself in the shoes of the test writers so that you can easily identify wrong answer choices
- ✓ showing you how to work through SAT problems the smart way
- ✓ teaching you how to guess smart on the toughest of problems

Concentration

Margaret, 17

"When I took the SAT, a boy next to me didn't take it. He sat there and scribbled on his desk. I could hardly focus. I know that it is partially my fault, but they should have asked him to leave…"

Females are experts at taking in the whole picture. When you walk down the hall in your school, you can simultaneously carry on a detailed conversation with your friend, see Ms. B in the hallway and make a mental note to talk to her after next period, jot down a reminder on your notebook to hit the library after school, and glance back at the scuffle in the hall. This is not to imply that you are scatterbrained; on the contrary, you are able to give each of these tasks the appropriate amount of attention. The female ability to multitask is highly valued throughout our society. However, being aware of the whole picture or the activities around us does not work to our advantage on an exam that requires our total concentration. Too often, things that occur in the testing environment, personal concerns, or worries about the test distract girls from giving their full attention to the test.

What Distracts You?

Certain things that occur in the testing environment can be distracting to girls who tend to focus outwardly. If you are the kind of person who is very social and very aware of your surroundings, you may find it difficult to ignore what others are doing in the testing room. Other girls are distracted by personal issues or discomforts. In the middle of a section you may find yourself worrying about what you have to do after the test or about how uncomfortable you are sitting in that small desk. Still other girls are distracted by The Test—the knowledge of what test scores mean, the need to do well and the challenges to that end, the time pressure, or the duration of the exam.

Concentration Solutions

Determining what distracts you in a test setting is the first part of increasing your ability to fully concentrate on test day. In addition, your ability to see the whole picture is advantageous when put to proper use. Solution #6: Concentrate will help you develop your concentration for test day. You will learn how to create your personal testing space. You will learn how to get rid of the distractions that you have control over and how to cope with the ones that are out of your control. You'll learn how to focus throughout the test, and you'll also have the opportunity to try out different focusing techniques to see which ones work best for you. Practice your concentration strategies, and you will be able to call upon them as needed on test day.

Solution #6: Concentrate will help you close the gender gap by

- ✓ helping you learn to deal with distractions that come from others, yourself, and the test
- ✓ showing you how to create your own personal testing space to encourage total concentration
- ✓ providing you with techniques for refocusing your mind throughout the test

NERVES

Kaitlyn, 16

"Well, first of all, tests freak me out to begin with, and taking the SATs was, for me, one of the scariest things ever! I overthought everything and I think that made me do worse."

For many girls, taking the SAT is nerve-racking. Some girls get nervous for most major tests; others have never experienced test jitters before encountering the SAT. There are myriad studies on the effect of nervousness and anxiety on test performance. As I'm sure you could guess, most studies indicate that anxiety lowers test scores and that girls report experiencing test anxiety more often than boys do.

The main reason girls give for getting nervous about the SAT is that they tend to focus on what the SAT means to their future. These thoughts add undue anxiety, making it difficult for some girls to concentrate or remain calm on test day. Over the years, my female students have expressed feeling both internal and external pressure to do well. Internally, they want to and need to do well to get into the school of their dreams. At the same time, they feel pressure to do well from teachers, counselors, peers, and parents. Many girls, even after prepping and gaining confidence in their SAT test-taking abilities, still get nervous the morning of the test. Girls report "drawing a blank" or "freezing up" on the test and resorting to older, less effective test-taking strategies. After taking a practice test during a course, one of my students said, "I know it was only a practice test, but once the proctor started timing us, I panicked and couldn't concentrate." For the rest of the course, she worked not only on learning the techniques, but also on learning how to manage her nervous energy.

The release of adrenaline is your body's natural reaction to being challenged to perform in a high-stakes setting. And it is not a bad thing. If you've performed on stage or in a major competition, you are familiar with how increased adrenaline can actually strengthen your performance. Adrenaline puts you in a heightened state of awareness—not a bad place to be when you are taking a major exam. However, an excess of adrenaline can make it difficult to concentrate. Your goal, when it comes to getting nervous, is to allow yourself to get *a little* nervous—just enough to heighten your focus. Solution #7: Be a Little Nervous will help you learn how to hold on to good adrenaline while letting the excess go.

More Than Just Butterflies

If you have taken the PSAT or SAT and your results were not as good as you would have hoped, how has that made you feel? Have you experienced a loss of confidence because of your results? If so, you're not alone.

Studies indicate that girls tend to blame themselves when they do not do as well as expected. Many girls who are typically self-assured find that their confidence is challenged by their experience with the SAT. "Why can't I understand this passage? I read voraciously." "Why am I having trouble with this math question? I love math!" The jolt of feeling unsure of an answer choice or not knowing which way to do a problem when these areas have never been an issue in the past can create a tremendous amount of anxiety and doubt.

For some, the SAT seems to bring out more than simple test jitters; for many, it brings about a loss of confidence in one's abilities. Why some girls respond this way is not clear—it may be because of the high-stakes nature of this exam, or because many people still perceive it as an intelligence test. Whatever the reason, many girls have expressed to me feeling more insecure overall based on their experience with the SAT. "I have to say that the night before the SAT I could not sleep, even though I know, it really doesn't count for anything yet (I was taking it as a sophomore). I get straight A's and like to consider myself intelligent, but the SATs will probably not represent that."

Losing confidence in your ability to do well on the SAT often becomes a vicious circle. If you do not do as well as expected on the SAT, and then blame yourself for your performance, you feel less confident the next time you take the test. Feeling less confidence while taking the test translates into a loss of concentration, second-guessing, increased test anxiety, etc. And, of course, these responses to your insecurities lead back to lower test scores.

Who Are You?

I had a professor once who liked to talk about "the imposter theory." He said that even as we go through our lives accomplishing this and that, striving to do our best, somewhere deep down inside we are convinced that we are merely imposters, and that, sooner or later, someone is going to realize that we have no idea what we are doing. I think some girls react to less-than-stellar SAT scores this way. They feel that "the test scores must be right, I'm no good at math, and my grades all these years have been a fluke." In other words, they feel like imposters: Finally, someone—or in this case, the SAT—has caught on to them.

I Know I Can

One student wrote on her survey: "It's hard to take the SAT. There's so much pressure on this one test...I don't think it really does a good job of reflecting my academic ability. I also think I would be capable of doing a good job in a good college—regardless of my scores." She's right—you will do well in college, regardless of your SAT scores. And the more you learn about the SAT, the better you will do on the test. Studies clearly indicate that students who prep—particularly girls—not only score higher but also feel more confident about their ability to take the SAT. As one Princeton Review student said at the end of her course, "I had no clue what to expect on the real SAT. I'm now confident in myself and know what to do when I'm confronted by certain situations."

If you've been hard on yourself about your PSAT or SAT scores, discover why the test was hard for you as opposed to blaming yourself for not doing as well as you should have. In addition, learn how to be a little nervous. Solution #7 will provide you with anxiety-reducers and confidence-builders that you can do before the test, during each section, and even after the test—like when you're on your college interviews!

Solution #7: Be a Little Nervous will help you close the gender gap by

- ✓ helping you determine which aspects of testing cause you to become anxious and to what degree
- ✓ teaching you to capture useful nervous energy and let the rest go
- ✓ providing you with anxiety-reducing techniques and affirmations to increase your sense of power over the test

Some Final Thoughts

I hope this chapter has shed some light on the issues that are causing the gender gap for most girls. Now it's time for you to decide which of these issues are affecting your test performance. Chapter 3 will help you explore each area further. It's filled with worksheets and questionnaires designed to help you identify what makes the SAT difficult for you. Once you've determined which areas of the test challenge you most, you can start building your skills—and confidence—by working through the seven solutions to the gender gap.

Jackie, 16

"I hate SATs. It was my least favorite way ever to spend a Saturday morning."

Chapter 3
WHAT YOU SAY

Regardless of what the research says, *you* are the one taking the test. You are the one working to get into college. What you think and what you feel about the test are far more important than anyone else's opinion.

Is This an Issue for You?

Each of the following brief questionnaires is designed to give you a quick snapshot of your feelings regarding the seven major issues that contribute to the gender gap. Complete each of the following questionnaires as instructed. Then, based on your responses, complete the appropriate worksheets on each area that poses a challenge to you. There are no right or wrong answers to these questionnaires; they are merely tools to help you examine each aspect of the test.

Test Overall Questionnaire

For each statement below, mark whether you agree or disagree. After considering all of the statements, add up the marks in each column. If your Agree total is greater than or equal to your Disagree total, you need to work on your knowledge of the test overall. Complete the Test Overall worksheet to further examine this issue.

Statement	Agree	Disagree
I do better on a test when I know who is testing me and what is expected.		
I have difficulty concentrating on a test that is several hours long.		
If you've taken a PSAT or SAT:		
I was confused when taking the PSAT/SAT because I didn't understand its structure.		
I did not do well on the PSAT/SAT because I just didn't know what the test writers wanted.		
I had trouble telling whether a question was supposed to be easy or hard on the PSAT/SAT.		
Total:		

MATH QUESTIONNAIRE

For each statement below, mark whether you agree or disagree. After considering all of the statements, add up the marks in each column. If your Agree total is greater than or equal to your Disagree total, you need to work on your SAT math skills. Complete the Math worksheet to further examine this issue.

Statement	Agree	Disagree
I don't like math.		
I am not good at math.		
I have trouble doing math problems when I am being timed.		
If you've taken a PSAT or SAT:		
I found the math portion of the PSAT/SAT harder than I had expected.		
I had trouble deciding how to solve many of the problems on the Math portion of the PSAT/SAT.		
I had trouble concentrating during the Math portion of the PSAT/SAT because of the time constraints.		
I scored lower than expected on the Math portion of the PSAT/SAT.		
Total:		

VERBAL QUESTIONNAIRE

For each statement below, mark whether you agree or disagree. After considering all of the statements, add up the marks in each column. If your Agree total is greater than or equal to of your Disagree total, you need to work on your SAT verbal skills. Complete the Verbal worksheet to further examine this issue.

Statement	Agree	Disagree
I don't like to read.		
I don't like English class.		
I have a weak vocabulary.		
I do not do well on tests in which I must read a lot under timed conditions.		
If you've taken a PSAT or SAT:		
I found the Verbal portion of the PSAT/SAT harder than I had expected.		
I found the vocabulary on the PSAT/SAT to be very difficult.		
I had trouble concentrating during the Verbal portion of the PSAT/SAT because of the time constraints.		
I scored lower than expected on the Verbal portion of the PSAT/SAT.		
Total:		

Timing Questionnaire

For each statement below, mark whether you agree or disagree. After considering all of the statements, add up the marks in each column. If your Agree total is greater than or equal to your Disagree total, you need to work on timing. Complete the Timing worksheet to further examine this issue.

Statement	Agree	Disagree
I feel rushed when I take a test.		
If I know a test is being timed, I can't concentrate.		
I am much more accurate if I can work at my own pace during a test.		
If you've taken a PSAT or SAT:		
I had trouble finishing the Verbal portion of the PSAT/SAT.		
I had trouble finishing the Math portion of the PSAT/SAT.		
I had trouble concentrating during the PSAT/SAT because I felt rushed.		
I know I would have scored better if I had had more time on the PSAT/SAT.		
Total:		

Assertiveness and Guessing Questionnaire

For each statement below, mark whether you agree or disagree. After considering all of the statements, add up the marks in each column. If your Agree total is greater than or equal to your Disagree total, you need to work on assertiveness and guessing. Complete the Assertiveness and Guessing worksheet to further examine this issue.

Statement	Agree	Disagree
I don't like to cut corners when I work on test questions.		
I prefer to keep working on a problem until I solve it.		
When I take a test, I only answer the question when I'm sure I know the answer.		
If you've taken a PSAT or SAT:		
During the PSAT/SAT, I didn't know when to guess and when to leave a question blank.		
During the PSAT/SAT, I would continue to work on a problem that I was having trouble with instead of guessing.		
During the PSAT/SAT, I generally solved problems the long way even when I saw a shortcut.		
If I tried to solve a problem on the PSAT/SAT and didn't find the answer, I left it blank.		
Total:		

Concentration Questionnaire

For each statement below, mark whether you agree or disagree. After considering all of the statements, add up the marks in each column. If your Agree total is greater than or equal to your Disagree total, you need to work on concentration. Complete the Concentration worksheet to further examine this issue.

Statement	Agree	Disagree
I have trouble focusing during most tests.		
I have trouble focusing on standardized tests.		
If you've taken a PSAT or SAT:		
I had trouble concentrating on the Verbal portion of the PSAT/SAT.		
I had trouble concentrating on the Math portion of the PSAT/SAT.		
I was distracted by other test takers when I took the PSAT/SAT.		
During the PSAT/SAT, I found it hard to focus on the problem I was on because I kept thinking about problems I had already completed.		
Total:		

NERVES QUESTIONNAIRE

For each statement below, mark whether you agree or disagree. After considering all of the statements, add up the marks in each column. If your Agree total is greater than or equal to your Disagree total, you need to work on harnessing your nervous energy. Complete the Nerves worksheet to further examine this issue.

Statement	Agree	Disagree
I get nervous before most tests.		
I feel insecure when I take most tests.		
I can't eat before I take a major exam.		
If you've taken a PSAT or SAT:		
I felt nervous before beginning the PSAT/SAT.		
I felt nervous throughout the entire PSAT/SAT.		
I felt out of control during the PSAT/SAT.		
Total:		

NOW WHAT?

Based on your results, complete the worksheets that correspond to the areas you need to work on (or complete all worksheets if you wish). The worksheets are designed for you to record your perspective on each topic. When you have completed the worksheets, read the Part II Introduction to see how best to use your worksheets in conjunction with the second half of this book.

TEST OVERALL WORKSHEET

What aspects of the SAT are hardest for you? Is it not knowing what's expected of you? Is it not understanding the structure of the test? Describe your experiences on the PSAT/SAT or other standardized tests. What do you want to learn about the test in general?

What I have experienced . . .

Describe my experiences on the PSAT/SAT (or other exams) and any related concerns:

What do I find difficult or challenging about the PSAT/SAT?

What I want to know . . .

When I took the PSAT/SAT, what rules or expectations were unclear to me?

What do I want to know about the SAT in general?

Solution #1: Know the Test (Chapter 4)

MATH WORKSHEET

What aspects of the Math portion of the SAT are hardest for you? Are you good at math but bad at SAT math? Does all math give you trouble? Describe your experience with the Math portion of the SAT or with other math exams. What do you want to learn about the Math SAT?

What I have experienced . . .

Describe my experiences taking the PSAT/SAT Math section (or similar math exams):

What types of math questions do I like and dislike, both on the SAT and in school?

What I want to know . . .

When I took the PSAT/SAT, what types of math problems did I not know how to solve?

What do I want to learn in Math?

Solution #2: Do the Math (Chapter 5)

Prerequisite: Chapter 4

VERBAL WORKSHEET

What makes the Verbal section of the SAT hard for you? Is it the different types of questions on each section? Is it the vocabulary? Describe your experiences with the Verbal section or the SAT or with other verbal exams. What do you want to learn about the Verbal portion of the SAT?

What I have experienced . . .

Describe my experiences taking the Verbal PSAT/SAT (or similar verbal exams):

What are my strengths and weaknesses regarding verbal skills, including vocabulary?

What I want to know . . .

When I took the Verbal PSAT/SAT, what types of verbal problems did I not know how to solve?

What do I want to learn in Verbal?

Solution #3: Get Verbal (Chapter 6)

Prerequisite: Chapter 5

Timing Worksheet

Do you find it difficult to do as many problems as you think you should when a test is timed? Do you have trouble concentrating because you're worrying about the time? Describe your experiences with timed exams, including the SAT. What do you want to learn about timing and pacing on the SAT?

What I have experienced . . .

Describe my experiences taking the PSAT/SAT (or similar exams) regarding the time constraints:

How do I think the time constraints on the SAT has/will affect my test taking?

What I want to know . . .

When I took the PSAT/SAT, what bothered me most about the time constraints?

What do I want to learn about timing and pacing on the SAT?

Solution #4: Take Your Time (Chapter 7)

Prerequisite: Chapters 4, 5, and 6

Assertiveness and Guessing Worksheet

Do you feel comfortable guessing on the SAT? Do you take shortcuts when you see them? Describe the way you like to solve problems on the SAT, and how you typically guess. What do you want to learn about solving problems efficiently and guessing on the SAT?

What I have experienced . . .

Describe how I solved most questions on the PSAT/SAT (or similar exam):

Describe how I tended to guess (or not guess) on the PSAT/SAT (or similar exam):

What I want to know . . .

What do I want to learn about how to solve problems efficiently on the PSAT/SAT?

What do I want to learn about how to guess on the PSAT/SAT?

Solution #5: Work Smart, Guess Smart (Chapter 8)

Prerequisite: Chapters 4, 5, and 6

Concentration Worksheet

Do you have trouble concentrating on the SAT? On other tests? Are you distracted by what's going on around you? Describe your experiences regarding concentration on tests like the SAT. What do you want to learn to help you concentrate on the SAT?

What I have experienced . . .

Describe my experiences taking the PSAT/SAT (or similar exam) regarding concentration:

What do I find most distracting during tests like the SAT?

What I want to know . . .

What would help me concentrate during the SAT?

What do I want to learn about concentrating?

Solution #6: Concentrate (Chapter 9)

Nerves Worksheet

Do your nerves get the best of you during tests like the SAT? Are you nervous the morning of the test, the day before the test, or the entire week before the test? Describe any testing situations in which your nerves or anxiety affected your performance. What do you want to learn that would help you remain calm on the SAT?

What I have experienced . . .

Describe my experiences taking the PSAT/SAT (or similar exams) regarding nerves and anxiety:

What makes me most nervous before or during tests like the SAT?

What I want to know . . .

What would help me remain relaxed during the SAT?

What else do I want to know about managing test anxiety?

Solution #7: Be A Little Nervous (Chapter 10)

PART II

Solution Guide and Study Plan

SOLVING THE GENDER GAP

Part I gave you a good idea of what the gender gap is all about. In addition, your work in Chapter 3 should have helped you zero in on the areas affecting your personal test performance. Now it's time for some solutions.

Each chapter of Part II contains a solution to one of the seven problems behind the gender gap. Within each chapter, you will find information, techniques, and exercises to help you solve that problem. While some chapters can be worked through at any time, others should be approached in order. In addition, you will return to some chapters multiple times, while others you may only have to read once.

To be as prepared as you can for the SAT, I recommend you work through Chapter 4: Know the Test, Chapter 5: Do the Math, Chapter 6: Get Verbal, Chapter 7: Take Your Time, and Chapter 8: Work Smart, Guess Smart. Chapter 9: Concentrate, and Chapter 10: Be A Little Nervous, are optional chapters but do contain some great tips and techniques that you might find useful, even if these areas are not major concerns for you. The following pages contain guides to the contents of each of the seven "solutions" chapters. These pages will make it easy for you to find what you need, when you need it, within each chapter.

After the content guides, you will find several suggested practice plans. How you work through the rest of this book has a great deal to do with how much time you have to prepare for the SAT. I have included an **extended practice plan** for those of you who have three months (or more) to prepare, a **turbo practice plan** for those of you who have eight to ten weeks to prepare, an **intensive practice plan** for those of you who have four to six weeks to prepare, and a **crammer practice plan** for those of you who have only three weeks (or fewer—yikes!) to prepare. I've also included a practice plan chart for you to fill out so that you can personalize your prep plan. Note that to complete your practice plans, you'll need to have access to practice SAT questions, preferably real ones. I strongly recommend that you purchase the book *10 Real SATs*, published by the College Board and widely available in bookstores and at the College Board's Web site.

Take a look at each of the chapter content guides, then spend some time developing your personal practice plan. Once you're ready, start beating the gender gap!

SOLUTION #1: KNOW THE TEST

Chapter 4, the first chapter of Part II, contains Solution #1: Know the Test. Don't skip this chapter! Chapter 4 will tell you all about how the test is structured and who writes the questions, and provides you with important techniques that you will use throughout the SAT. You'll find a guide to Chapter 4 on the next page.

- Know the Structure of the SAT
- Order of Difficulty
- Do Fewer Questions, Get a Higher Score
- Who Writes the Test? How Do They Do It?
- Process of Elimination
- Hard Question Strategies
- Guessing
- Jane Bloggs

SOLUTION #2: DO THE MATH

After you work through Chapter 4, you will be ready to learn specific techniques for both the Math and Verbal portions of the SAT. You may work through the math and verbal chapters in whichever order you prefer. If you have time, concentrate on a single technique in one of these chapters, and stick with it until you've mastered it, before moving on. Chapter 5: Do the Math will review some SAT math basics, then teach you techniques for solving arithmetic, algebra, and geometry problems. You will also learn how to solve Quantitative Comparison math problems and defeat word problems by taking them apart. Prerequisite (i.e., what you need to do before you do this chapter): Solution #1: Know the Test (Chapter 4). Here is a guide to Chapter 5:

- Arithmetic
- Averages
- Ratios
- Percents
- Word Problems, Piece by Piece
- Algebra
- Plug in the Answers (PITA)
- Plug in Your Own Number
- No Variables, No Numbers
- Jane Bloggs
- Geometry
- Quant Comp
- Grid-Ins

Solution #3: Get Verbal

Remember that you can work through the math and verbal chapters in whichever order you want, as long as you have first completed Chapter 4: Know the Test. If you have the time, do one type of verbal problem at a time, then practice the techniques for that type of problem before going on to the next. Chapter 6: Get Verbal will teach you how to solve sentence completions and analogies plus give you an effective method for dealing with critical reading. In addition, Chapter 6 will also point you toward the best way to build your SAT vocabulary. Prerequisite: Solution #1: Know the Test (Chapter 4). Here is a guide to Chapter 6:

- **SAT Vocabulary**
- **Sentence Completions**
- **Analogies**
- **Critical Reading**
- **Critical Working**

Solution #4: Take Your Time

On the SAT, timing is critical. However, you should not begin the timing chapter until you have learned and practiced all the techniques for at least one subject (math or verbal). If possible, practice math and verbal techniques without regard to timing at first. Then, once you've mastered each technique, you can begin to work on solving problems up to speed.

Chapter 7: Take Your Time is divided into two parts. Part I: Find Your Groove is designed to help you determine which questions you should do, which you should skip, and what scores you are currently on target for. Part II: Improve Your Groove is composed of various timed drills for you to use to practice your pacing strategy under timed conditions. You can do the Math portion of Part I as soon as you have mastered the math techniques in Chapter 5, and likewise for the Verbal portion of Part I. Part II requires that you set aside blocks of time to do uninterrupted timed work. You will return to the drills in Part II of this chapter throughout the weeks that lead up to the real SAT (see the suggested practice plans for ideas about how to schedule your time). Prerequisite: Solution #1: Know the Test (Chapter 4), Solution #2: Do the Math (Chapter 5), and/or Solution #3: Get Verbal (Chapter 6). Here is a guide to Chapter 7:

- Part I: Find Your Groove
- How Many Questions Should I Do?
- Finding Your Verbal Pacing Groove
- Finding Your Math Pacing Groove
- Part II: Improve Your Groove
- Five Minutes Left
- Full-Length Tests

Solution #5: Work Smart, Guess Smart

Chapter 8: Work Smart, Guess Smart consists of exercises and drills designed to help you hone your SAT test-taking approach. You'll work on solving questions efficiently as well as accurately, and you'll learn how and when to take a smart guess. Before you can benefit from this solution, you need to get all the math and verbal techniques under your belt. Prerequisite: Solution #1: Know the Test (Chapter 4), Solution #2: Do the Math (Chapter 5), and Solution #3: Get Verbal (Chapter 6). Here is a guide to Chapter 8:

- You Write the Test
- You Be the Critic
- Work Smart
- Guess Smart
- Are You SAT-Smart Yet?

Solution #6: Concentrate

If you ever have trouble concentrating, this is the chapter for you. Even if concentration is typically not a big issue for you, you may want to flip through this chapter for ideas of what to do if something unexpectedly distracts you during your test. You can work through Chapter 9: Concentrate at any time—use it to take a break from all that intense technique work you have to do in the earlier chapters. Here is a guide to Chapter 9:

- Create Your Personal Testing Space
- No More Distractions from Others
- No More Distractions from Yourself
- No More Distractions from the Test
- Back into Focus
- Don't Be Late, Lost, or Lacking

Solution #7: Be a Little Nervous

If you're worried about anxiety on test day, or simply want to learn some quick stress relievers just in case, don't miss this chapter. It will teach you to channel your nervous energy by getting psyched for the exam, plus describe exercises and tension breakers to prevent or reduce harmful test anxiety. You can work through this chapter at any time during your preparation. However, if test anxiety is a big issue for you, focus on this chapter a few weeks before the test so that you have enough time to practice the techniques. Here is a guide to Chapter 10:

- Get Psyched
- Feel Good on the Spot
- Don't Take It Too Seriously
- Ten-Second Tension Breakers

Read Me the Week Before the SAT

This final chapter contains everything you need for the day of the SAT. It contains a Test Day Checklist, a collection of focusing techniques, space for you to write down your favorite tension breakers, plus math and verbal review pages and warm-up drills. Read through this chapter the week before the SAT to get a heads up as to what to expect and what you'll need to bring. Here's a guide to Chapter 11:

- Day of Test Checklist
- Concentration Techniques and Stress Reducers I Plan to Use
- Get-Psyched Exercise
- My Personal Testing Space
- My Math Strategy
- My Verbal Strategy

Your Practice Plan

When are you taking the SAT? Next fall? Next month? Next week? The amount of time you have will significantly affect how you prepare for the test. To develop your own practice plan, first look at the following suggested plans. Read through them and either use one of them as is or create your own plan in the space provided.

Set Your Practice Schedule

To get the most out of your SAT prep, design a practice schedule that works for you. If you have tons of schoolwork, schedule a little SAT prep every day. If you have a lot of after-school commitments and a fair amount of time before you are going to take the SAT, set aside a block of time every weekend for SAT prep. In addition, only you know how you study best. If you like to work on something for hours until you totally master it, work that time into your schedule. If you learn best when you study for short periods, plan accordingly.

Pick a Partner

Many girls find it very helpful to study with someone. If you're one of those girls, try to find a friend to prep with. The two of you can work together on the techniques and drills and take turns teaching the concepts and problems to each other. You will both benefit from the experience come test day.

EXTENDED PREP PLAN

Weeks To Go	Option One	Option Two	Option Three
12	• Do Chapter 4: Know the Test	• Do Chapter 4: Know the Test	• Do Chapter 4: Know the Test
11	• Do half of Chapter 5: Do the Math OR Chapter 6: Get Verbal • Practice techniques	• Do half of Chapter 5: Do the Math OR Chapter 6: Get Verbal • Practice techniques	• Do half of Chapter 5: Do the Math OR Chapter 6: Get Verbal • Practice techniques
10	• Do other half of chapter • Practice techniques • Decide if you need add'l prep in the subject you just learned (from *Cracking the SAT*)	• Do other half of chapter • Practice techniques • Do Part I of Chapter 7: Take Your Time, focusing on the subject you just studied (either math or verbal)	• Do other half of chapter • Practice techniques • Do Chapter 9: Concentrate
9	• Do half of Chapter 6: Get Verbal OR Chapter 5: Do the Math • Practice techniques • Work with your Vocab Stash	• Do half of Chapter 6: Get Verbal OR Chapter 5: Do the Math • Practice techniques • Decide if you need add'l prep (from *Cracking the SAT*) • Work with your Vocab Stash	• Do half of Chapter 6: Get Verbal OR Chapter 5: Do the Math • Practice techniques • Decide if you need add'l prep (from *Cracking the SAT*) • Work with your Vocab Stash
8	• Do other half of chapter • Practice techniques • Decide if you need add'l prep (from *Cracking the SAT*)	• Do other half of chapter • Practice techniques • Do Part I of Chapter 7: Take Your Time for the subject you just studied	• Do other half of chapter • Practice techniques • Do Chapter 10: Be a Little Nervous
7	• Do Chapter 7: Take Your Time, Part I • Practice techniques • Work with your Vocab Stash	• Do Chapter 8: Work Smart, Guess Smart • Practice Techniques • Work with your Vocab Stash	• Do Chapter 7: Take Your Time, Part I • Practice Techniques • Work with your Vocab Stash

6	• Do Chapter 8: Work Smart, Guess Smart • Do some timed drills from Chapter 7, Part II	• Do some timed drills from Chapter 7, Part II Work on problem areas	• Do Chapter 8: Work Smart, Guess Smart • Practice techniques
5	• Do Chapter 9: Concentrate • Do some timed drills from Chapter 7, Part II • Work with your Vocab Stash	• Do Chapter 9: Concentrate • Do some timed drills from Chapter 7, Part II • Work with your Vocab Stash	• Do timed drills from Chapter 7, Part II • Work on problem areas • Work with your Vocab Stash
4	• Do Chapter 10: Be a Little Nervous • Take a full-length test • Work on problem areas	• Do Chapter 10: Be a Little Nervous • Take a full-length test • Work on problem areas	• Take a full-length test • Work on problem areas • Practice some concentration techniques
3	• Do some timed drills • Take a full-length test • Work on problem areas • Practice some concentration techniques • Work with your Vocab Stash	• Do some timed drills • Take a full-length test • Work on problem areas • Practice some concentration techniques • Work with your Vocab Stash	• Do some timed drills • Take a full-length test • Work on problem areas • Practice some anxiety-reducing techniques • Work with your Vocab Stash
2	• Review all techniques • Take a full-length test • Practice some anxiety-reducing techniques • Work with your Vocab Stash	• Review all techniques • Take a full-length test • Practice some anxiety-reducing techniques • Work with your Vocab Stash	• Review all techniques • Take a full-length test • Work on problem areas • Work with your Vocab Stash
1	• Take a full-length test • Review • Read Chapter 11 • Get stuff together for SAT morning	• Take a full-length test • Review • Read Chapter 11 • Get stuff together for SAT morning	• Take a full-length test • Review • Read Chapter 11 • Get stuff together for SAT morning
SAT	Go for it!	Go for it!	Go for it!

TURBO PREP PLAN

Weeks To Go	10-Week Turbo	9-Week Turbo	8-Week Turbo
10	• Do Chapter 4: Know the Test		
9	• Do Chapter 5: Do the Math OR Chapter 6: Get Verbal • Practice techniques	• Do Chapter 4: Know the Test	
8	• Do Chapter 6: Get Verbal OR Chapter 5: Do the Math • Practice techniques • Decide if you need add'l prep (from *Cracking the SAT*) • Work with your Vocab Stash	• Do Chapter 5: Do the Math OR Chapter 6: Get Verbal • Practice techniques	• Do Chapter 4: Know the Test
7	• Do Chapter 7: Take Your Time, Part I • Practice techniques • Do some timed drills from Chapter 7, Part II	• Do Chapter 6: Get Verbal OR Chapter 5: Do the Math • Practice techniques • Decide if you need add'l prep (from *Cracking the SAT*) • Work with your Vocab Stash	• Do Chapter 5: Do the Math OR Chapter 6: Get Verbal • Practice techniques • Decide if you need additional prep (from *Cracking the SAT*)
6	• Do Chapter 8: Work Smart, Guess Smart • Do some timed drills from Chapter 7, Part II	• Do Chapter 7: Take Your Time, Part I • Practice Techniques	• Do Chapter 6: Get Verbal OR Chapter 5: Do the Math • Practice techniques • Decide if you need add'l prep (from *Cracking the SAT*) • Work with your Vocab Stash

5	• Do Chapter 9: Concentrate • Do some timed drills from Chapter 7, Part II • Work with your Vocab Stash	• Do Chapter 8: Work Smart, Guess Smart • Do timed drills from Chapter 7, Part II • Work with your Vocab Stash	• Practice techniques • Do Chapter 7: Take Your Time, Part I • Do some timed drills from Chapter 7, Part II • Work with your Vocab Stash
4	• Do Chapter 10: Be a Little Nervous • Do some timed drills from Chapter 7, Part II • Take a full-length test	• Do Chapter 9: Concentrate • Do timed drills from Chapter 7, Part II • Work on problem areas • Work with your Vocab Stash	• Do Chapter 8: Work Smart, Guess Smart • Do timed drills from Chapter 7, Part II • Work on problem areas
3	• Take a full-length test • Work on problem areas Practice some concentration techniques • Do timed drills • Work with your Vocab Stash	• Do Chapter 10: Be a Little Nervous • Take a full-length test • Do timed drills from Chapter 7, Part II • Work with your Vocab Stash	• Take a full-length test • Do Chapter 9: Concentrate • Do Chapter 10: Be a Little Nervous • Do timed drills • Work with your Vocab Stash
2	• Review all techniques • Take a full-length test • Practice some anxiety-reducing techniques • Work with your Vocab Stash	• Review all techniques • Take a full-length test • Practice concentration and anxiety-reducing techniques • Do timed drills	• Take a full-length test • Practice concentration and anxiety-reducing techniques • Do timed drills • Work with your Vocab Stash
1	• Review all techniques • Take a full-length test • Read Chapter 11 • Get stuff together for SAT morning	• Review all techniques • Take a full-length test • Read Chapter 11 • Get stuff together for SAT morning	• Review all techniques • Take a full-length test • Read Chapter 11 • Get stuff together for SAT morning
SAT	Go for it!	Go for it!	Go for it!

INTENSIVE PREP PLAN

Weeks To Go	6-Week Intensive	5-Week Intensive	4-Week Intensive
6	• Do Chapter 4: Know the Test • Do Chapter 5: Do the Math OR Chapter 6: Get Verbal • Practice techniques • Do Part I of Chapter 7: Take Your Time, focusing on the subject you just studied		
5	• Do Chapter 6: Get Verbal OR Chapter 5: Do the Math • Practice techniques • Do Part I of Chapter 7: Take Your Time, focusing on the subject you just studied • Decide if you need add'l prep (from *Cracking the SAT*)	• Do Chapter 4: Know the Test • Do Chapter 5: Do the Math OR Chapter 6: Get Verbal • Practice techniques • Do Part I of Chapter 7: Take Your Time, focusing on the subject you just studied	
4	• Do Chapter 8: Work Smart, Guess Smart • Do timed drills from Chapter 7, Part II • Practice techniques • Work with your Vocab Stash	• Do Chapter 6: Get Verbal OR Chapter 5: Do the Math • Practice techniques • Do Part I of Chapter 7: Take Your Time, focusing on the subject you just studied • Decide if you need add'l prep (from *Cracking the SAT*) • Work with your Vocab Stash	• Do Chapter 4: Know the Test • Do Chapter 5: Do the Math OR Chapter 6: Get Verbal • Practice techniques • Do Part I of Chapter 7: Take Your Time, focusing on the subject you just studied

3	• Take a full-length test • Do Chapter 9: Concentrate • Practice and do timed drills • Work with your Vocab Stash	• Do Chapter 8: Work Smart, Guess Smart • Do timed drills from Chapter 7, Part II • Practice techniques • Take a full-length test • Work with your Vocab Stash	• Do Chapter 6: Get Verbal OR Chapter 5: Do the Math • Practice techniques • Do Part I of Chapter 7: Take Your Time, focusing on the subject you just studied • Work with your Vocab Stash
2	• Take a full-length test • Do Chapter 10: Be a Little Nervous • Practice concentration and anxiety-reducing techniques • Do timed drills • Work with your Vocab Stash	• Take a full-length test • Do Chapter 9: Concentrate • Practice and do timed drills • Do Chapter 10: Be a Little Nervous • Practice concentration and anxiety-reducing techniques • Work with your Vocab Stash	• Do Chapter 8: • Work Smart, Guess Smart • Do timed drills from Chapter 7, Part II • Practice techniques • Take a full-length test • Do Chapters 9: Concentrate and Chapter 10: Be a Little Nervous, time permitting • Work with your Vocab Stash
1	• Review all techniques • Take a full-length test • Read Chapter 11 • Get stuff together for SAT morning	• Review all techniques • Take a full-length test • Read Chapter 11 • Get stuff together for SAT morning	• Review all techniques • Take a full-length test • Read Chapter 11 • Get stuff together for SAT morning
SAT	Go for it!	Go for it!	Go for it!

CRAMMER PRACTICE PLAN

Weeks To Go	3-Week Crammer
3	• Do Chapter 4: Know the Test • Do Chapter 5: Do the Math OR Chapter 6: Get Verbal • Practice techniques • Do Part I of Chapter 7: Take Your Time, focusing on the subject you just studied • Do timed drills from Chapter 7, Part II
2	• Do Chapter 6: Get Verbal OR Chapter 5: Do the Math • Practice techniques • Do Part I of Chapter 7: Take Your Time, focusing on the subject you just studied • Do Chapter 8: Work Smart, Guess Smart • Do timed drills • Work with your Vocab Stash
1	• Review all techniques • Take a full-length test • Work with your Vocab Stash • Read Chapters 9 and 10 (time permitting) if relevant • Read Chapter 11 • Get stuff together for SAT morning
SAT	Go for it!

MY PERSONAL PREP PLAN

Weeks To Go	To Do This Week
SAT	

Chapter 4
Know the Test

Solution #1: Know the Test

To overcome the gender gap and score your best on the SAT, you must first know the SAT. This chapter teaches you all about the structure of the SAT and introduces you to the ETS test writers. In addition, it will show you important techniques that work for multiple-choice tests in general—and the SAT in particular.

Specifically, you will learn

- how the SAT is structured and how its Order of Difficulty can help you
- why doing fewer questions will get you a higher score
- who writes the SAT, how they do it, and why that matters to you
- how to use Process of Elimination (POE)
- who Jane Bloggs is and how to avoid her favorite trap answers

Know the Structure of the SAT

What Are SATs Made Of?

The SAT consists of seven sections: two 30-minute Math sections plus a 15-minute Math section, two 30-minute Verbal sections plus a 15-minute Verbal section, and one Experimental section. While you and all the students in your testing center will be taking the same test, you will not all be taking the same version. Different versions of the test have the sections in different orders, so don't worry if the person next to you turns the page long before you do—she may be on a Math section that only has two questions on the first page, while you are doing a page full of sentence completions.

The Experimental Section

Remember that ETS tests future SAT questions by including an Experimental section as part of your SAT. Think about that for a minute: You paid them for the privilege of taking the SAT, and now you get to be a guinea pig for 30 minutes? There is no way to determine which section is the Experimental section, and you should never blow off a section just because you think it might be experimental. Just know that it's there, and that if you encounter a section that's a little weird or a lot harder than you anticipated, it's probably the Experimental section.

Order of Difficulty

Does the Following Scenario Sound Familiar?

> Okay, 30 minutes to do this Math section. Number 1. Wow, that's pretty easy. Am I missing something? No, that's gotta be it. Okay, number 2. Easy again. Hey, this test isn't so bad after all...Number 14. I don't get it. It could be this, or maybe they want that. Why can't I concentrate? This seems so much harder... number 20. What? I have no idea what they're even asking. Should I do this one or skip it? I better try it anyway...number 23. Well, that seems easy. It's got to be (C). Why did I think those other questions were so hard?

The first thing you need to know about the SAT is that the questions feel like they're getting harder because they are getting harder. Each group of questions on the SAT is lined up in an ascending order of difficulty. Test writers intentionally arrange the questions this way so that, in essence, a tester will work through each section until she reaches her "potential," and then she'll be unable to do any more questions. Notice in the above scenario the that tester found number 23 easy. But number 23 is one of the hardest math questions on the test. Do you think she got the question right? Probably not. On the first third of the section, easy questions have easy answers, so the obvious answer is probably right. However, beginning in the middle of the test, you need to be wary of the obvious answer. In the medium questions, sometimes the obvious answer is right and other times it's not. On the hardest questions, the obvious answer is almost always wrong.

Is It Always That Way?

Order of difficulty doesn't necessarily flow straight through a section. Rather, each type of question is arranged in increasing order of difficulty. For example, in the Verbal section, the first questions you encounter are sentence completions. Of those nine or ten sentence completions, the first three will be easy, the next three or four will be of medium difficulty, and the last three will be tough. In critical reading, sometimes the passages are given in order of difficulty, but that tendency doesn't always hold up. The questions themselves in critical reading are not given in order of difficulty. Open up your *10 Real SATs* (or *Cracking the SAT*) to a test, and then use the following charts to see how Order of Difficulty breaks down in each section.

MATH ORDER OF DIFFICULTY

	30-Minute Section	30-Minute Section		15-Minute Section
	25 Questions	25 Questions		10 Questions
	Problem Solving	Quantitative Comparisons	Grid-Ins	Problem Solving
EASY	1 2 3 4 5 6 7 8	1 2 3 4 5	(*first* 3) 16 17 18	1 2 3
MEDIUM	9 10 11 12 13 14 15 16 17	6 7 8 9 10	(*next* 4) 19 20 21 22	4 5 6 7
HARD	18 19 20 21 22 23 24 25	11 12 13 14 15	(*last* 3) 23 24 25	8 9 10

VERBAL ORDER OF DIFFICULTY

Note: There are a total of 78 verbal questions. The exact number per section varies slightly based on the number of critical reading questions in a given section.

<table>
<tr><th colspan="4">30-Minute Section</th><th colspan="3">30-Minute Section</th><th>15-Minute Section</th></tr>
<tr><th colspan="4">30–31 Questions</th><th colspan="3">35–36 Questions</th><th>12–13 Questions</th></tr>
<tr><th colspan="2">Sentence Completions</th><th>Analogies</th><th>Critical Reading</th><th>Sentence Completions</th><th>Analogies</th><th>Critical Reading</th><th>Critical Reading</th></tr>
<tr><td>EASY</td><td>1
2
3</td><td>(first 2)
10
11</td><td rowspan="3">16–30
or 31,
generally
not in
Order of
Difficulty</td><td>1
2
3</td><td>(first 4)
11
12
13
14</td><td rowspan="3">24–35
or 36,
generally
not in
Order of
Difficulty</td><td rowspan="3">1–12
or 13,
generally
not in
Order of
Difficulty</td></tr>
<tr><td>MEDIUM</td><td>4
5
6</td><td>(next 2)
12
13</td><td>4
5
6
7</td><td>(next 5)
15
16
17
18
19</td></tr>
<tr><td>HARD</td><td>7
8
9</td><td>(last 2)
14
15</td><td>8
9
10</td><td>(last 4)
20
21
22
23</td></tr>
</table>

How to Use Order of Difficulty

Knowing Order of Difficulty helps you (1) gauge how easy or difficult a particular question should be and (2) determine if you should answer or skip this question. On each question, you should first ask yourself, "How hard is this question according to ETS?"

- If it's an easy question, do it. Remember that easy questions have easy answers, so the obvious answer is probably right.
- If it's a medium question, do it unless it's really weird or you just don't know how. Be on your guard on medium questions. Sometimes the obvious answer is okay, and sometimes it's not.
- If it's a hard question, decide whether you are going to do it or skip it. If you are going to do it, remember that hard questions typically have hard answers, so the obvious answer is almost always wrong.

Do Fewer Questions, Get a Higher Score

All too often, test takers—girls and boys—begin each section of the SAT with the wrong goal—to finish the section. Perhaps the fact that the test is timed suggests that finishing is the main goal. However, striving to finish a section often leads to rushing and careless errors. To get your best SAT score, you must focus on accuracy first, then on speed. You don't have to do every question to get a good score.

For many of my female students, not trying to finish each section of the SAT is almost as stressful as is trying to finish each section. They worry about the questions they are not attempting, even though those questions are the hardest questions on the test—the ones everybody typically gets wrong anyway. They can see the careless errors they're making on easy questions as a result of their rushing, but they still have a hard time allowing themselves to slow down enough to be more accurate. If the idea of not doing all of the questions makes you a little tense, let me say this again: *You don't need to do every question to get the score you want.* In fact, the number of questions you need to get right to achieve your goal is probably lower than you think. And, by not attempting to do every question, you can slow down, work more accurately, and get more questions right.

But How Do I Know What to Skip?

By using Order of Difficulty, of course. Every question is worth the same on the SAT, no matter how difficult it is. If you get question 1 right, you get one point. If you get question 23 right, you also get one point, even though question 23 is a lot harder and takes a lot more time to do. Once you know how many questions you are going skip in each section—something you'll determine in Solution #4: Take Your Time (Chapter 7)—you should choose to skip that number of hard questions.

FEWER QUESTIONS, WHAT SCORE?

Just how many questions should you do (or not do) to get a good score? That depends, of course, on what a "good score" is for you. Let's look at some examples.

A score of 1200 puts you in the 79th percentile. To keep it simple, let's assume that you're shooting for a 600 in Math and a 600 in Verbal. To get a 600 in Math, you need a raw score of approximately 42; that translates to answering 42 out of 60 questions correctly (and leaving all the others blank). To get a 600 in Verbal, you need a raw score of approximately 54, or 54 out of 78 questions correct (all others blank).

THAT'S IT?

If you took a high school English test and got a 69 out of 100, would you consider that a good score? Not likely. But on the SAT, a Verbal score of 600 translates to getting about 69 percent of the questions right. If you only need to get 69 percent of the questions right to do well on this test, why rush to finish 100 percent of the questions and risk significantly increasing your margin of error?

HOW ABOUT ANOTHER SCORE?

To get a score of 1000 (500 Math and 500 Verbal), you need a raw score of approximately 35 in Verbal (35 out of 78 questions correct without errors), and a raw score of 28 in Math (28 out of 60 questions correct without errors). That means getting a little less than half the questions right. If you were to attempt just over half the questions, that would leave you room for a few mistakes, and give you a lot more time to get the questions you do attempt right.

WHY WOULD I SKIP A QUESTION?

If you determine in advance how many questions you are going to do per section, you can slow down and give yourself the time you need to get questions right. And getting questions right, not doing lots of questions, is what will raise your SAT score. In Math, if you attempt to answer all the questions in a 30-minute Math section, you'll only have about 1.2 minutes to answer each question. However, if you decide ahead of time to skip just 5 questions, you give yourself an extra 6 minutes' work on the other 20 questions—and that's a lot of time on the SAT. Of course, if you're aiming for a really high score—say, in the 700s—you don't have as much leeway, so you'll probably only skip a few questions. After you learn and practice the math and verbal techniques, you will be able to determine the number of questions you should do on each section of the SAT. Solution #4: Take

Your Time will help you find the pace at which you work most accurately and efficiently. For now, just remember:

- To get the score you want, you only need to get a certain number of questions right.
- When you do fewer questions, you can slow down and get more questions right.
- Getting the questions you do right, and not simply doing more questions, will raise your score.
- Once you determine how many questions to skip, skip that number of hard questions.

WHO WRITES THE TEST? HOW DO THEY DO IT?

Just like the man behind the curtain in The *Wizard of Oz*, the people who write test questions for ETS are ordinary folks. Most are ETS employees who write questions for a living. Others are college students or freelance writers. In other words, SAT questions are written by real people just like you, me, your mom, or your Uncle Frank. To remind you of this, let's say that someone's Aunt Thelma is writing the test.

Now, when Aunt Thelma writes a test question, she first puts together the question, and then she writes a good, solid, correct answer. For example, let's say she's writing an Analogy question. First, she creates an appropriate analogy by defining the relationship between two words:

BOTANY : PLANTS :: *BOTANY is the study of PLANTS*

Then Aunt Thelma creates what she considers the right answer: BOTANY is the study of PLANTS—ZOOLOGY is the study of ANIMALS. Her question would now look something like this:

11. BOTANY : PLANTS ::

(A)
(B) zoology : animals
(C)
(D)
(E)

She's now written a question and created the correct answer choice. Before she can finish up and write more questions, she needs to create four wrong answer choices. To do this, she'll spend a little time creating one or two "runner up" answer choices—answer choices that look like they might be right but aren't. Since the two words in the question refer to plants, she creates answer choices that also refer to plants but don't reflect the right relationship. Now her question looks something like this:

11. BOTANY : PLANTS ::

(A) agriculture : herbs
(B) zoology : animals
(C)
(D)
(E) forestry : evergreens

Finally, she needs to fill in the rest of the wrong answer choices. Her final question looks like this:

11. BOTANY : PLANTS ::

(A) agriculture : herbs
(B) zoology : animals
(C) philosophy : books
(D) anthropology : religion
(E) forestry : evergreens

Why Does This Matter to Me?

Now, let's say you're taking the SAT. Without knowing anything about how Aunt Thelma writes analogies, you might attempt to solve her question like this:

BOTANY is to PLANTS. AGRICULTURE is to HERBS, ZOOLOGY is to ANIMALS, PHILOSOPHY is to BOOKS, ANTHROPOLOGY is to RELIGION, FORESTRY is to EVERGREENS... hmmm... well, AGRICULTURE and HERBS both deal with plants, and I know agriculture has to do with the growing of herbs, among other things, but it's not quite the same as BOTANY and PLANTS. ZOOLOGY and ANIMALS sounds possible, since zoology must have something to do with animals. PHILOSOPHY and BOOKS aren't really directly related, although when you take philosophy, you do read a lot of books. ANTHROPOLOGY and RELIGION have a little bit to do with each other, since you sometimes learn about the religions of past cultures when you study anthropology, but I don't know. FORESTRY and EVERGREENS relate to plants and caring for them so this might be the answer too. So, I guess it could be (A) or (B) or maybe (E), but probably (B).

ONE OUT OF FIVE AIN'T BAD

Even though you got to the correct answer, you spent far too much time considering the "rightness" of every answer choice. Instead, you need to remember the way Aunt Thelma wrote the question, and keep in mind that, on every question you read, every answer choice but one is wrong. Once you begin to read each answer choice suspiciously, you'll start to see how very wrong many answer choices can be. What should you do when you think an answer choice is wrong? Cross it out.

PROCESS OF ELIMINATION

Physically crossing off answers on the SAT is very empowering—it lets you do your work on paper and not in your head, it keeps you engaged and focused, and it reminds you that you are in control of the test, and not vice versa. When you decide an answer choice is wrong (and remember, most of them are!), grab your pencil and get it outta there. If you're not sure about an answer choice, leave it and read the next one. Once you have completed your first "pass" through the answer choices, you will have crossed off most of the bad answer choices. If you have a few choices left, consider each again, looking for what makes it wrong, not right. The process of identifying wrong answer choices and crossing them out is called Process of Elimination (POE). POE is one of the most powerful techniques at your disposal. From this day forward, whenever you take any multiple-choice test, use POE and cross off any wrong answer choice you encounter.

POE—EVEN WHEN YOU DON'T KNOW

Using POE can often get you moving toward the right answer even when you don't actually know the right answer. Try this:

1. What's the capital of Malawi?

You have no idea, do you? But now let's turn this into a multiple-choice question:

1. The capital of Malawi is

    (A) Washington, D.C.
    (B) Paris
    (C) Tokyo
    (D) London
    (E) Lilongwe

Even if you don't know what the capital of Malawi is, you certainly know that it is not Washington, Paris, Tokyo, or London. You can cross all those answers off, and choose the only one that's left: (E) Lilongwe. By using POE, you got to the correct answer choice simply by crossing off what was wrong. You'll be surprised by how many times you can get the right answer on the SAT simply by knowing what the answer cannot be. Let's see how POE can narrow down the choices on one of Aunt Thelma's SAT math questions:

10. What is the diameter of a circle with circumference 5?

Let's assume the only things you remember about circles are that the "circumference" is the outside of a circle and diameter is a line drawn from one side of the circle, through the circle's center, to the other side. Since there's no picture to help you on this question, you might want to draw a quick circle, and then draw a line through the center as the diameter. Is the line you drew for the diameter as long as the line you drew to create the circle? No. Therefore, you know that on this question, the diameter must be smaller than 5. Using only this information, look at the answer choices below and cross off the choices that are too big:

10. What is the diameter of a circle with circumference 5?

(A) $\frac{5}{\pi}$ (You should remember that π is about 3, or on the test you could use your calculator to find π. 5 divided by 3 is obviously smaller than 5)

(B) $\frac{10}{\pi}$ (10 divided by 3 is also smaller than 5)

(C) 5

(D) 5π (5 times something is bigger than 5)

(E) 10π (bigger still)

(C), (D), and (E) are all too big to be the diameter, so cross them off. Without doing any math, you just got rid of three answer choices. If you had no idea what to do next, you would still have a fifty-fifty chance of guessing the right answer to this question. Of course, before you take the SAT, you'll review how to find a diameter (there is a handy-dandy chart in the beginning of the Math section with formulas as a reminder). But even so, you don't want to waste your time doing unnecessary calculations like determining the values of (C), (D), and (E). Using POE saves you time and helps you avoid careless errors.

GUESSING—A SNEAK PEEK

Let's try POE on another non-SAT question:

1. The capital of Qatar is

(A) Paris
(B) Dukhan
(C) Tokyo
(D) Doha
(E) London

Using POE, you can easily eliminate (A), (C), and (E), even though you most likely have no idea what the capital of Qatar is. But now you are left with two possible answer choices. Should you guess? If this were an SAT question, absolutely.

BUT WHAT ABOUT THE GUESSING PENALTY?

The "guessing penalty" on the SAT is really more of a "not-guessing penalty." On the SAT, you get 1 point for every question you get right, and you lose $\frac{1}{4}$ of a point for every question you get wrong, with just a few exceptions (on Quant Comp math questions, which have only 4 possible answer choices instead of 5, you lose $\frac{1}{3}$ of a point for every wrong answer; on Grid-In math questions, you lose no points for a wrong answer). Since that's the case, you win, statistically speaking, every time you guess after eliminating just one wrong answer choice. Think of it this way: Imagine that your test proctor gives every tester one dollar for each correct answer (now there's a motivator!) but charges 25¢ for each wrong answer. Now imagine that the guy next to you just doesn't want to bother taking the test, so he colors in (C) on his bubble sheet for an entire 25-question section. Since there are five answer choices (for most SAT questions), the answer to 1 out of every 5 of the questions is likely to be (C), so the guy should get 5 out of 25 questions right just by chance. The proctor owes him $5 for the right answers. But since he got the rest of the questions wrong, he owes the proctor 20 times 25¢, or $5, for the wrong answers. In other words, it evens out. Nothing gained, nothing lost. Now imagine that someone magically crosses off one wrong answer choice for every question in the next 25-question section. The guy then proceeds to color in letters randomly on his bubble sheet for that section, avoiding the crossed-off answer. Now that he is only choosing from among four answer choices, he should get $\frac{1}{4}$ of the questions right. $\frac{1}{4}$ of 25 is about 6 questions. The proctor owes him $6 for that section. He got about 18 questions wrong, so he owes the proctor 18 times 25¢, or $4.50. He just made $1.50, just because one wrong answer choice was eliminated on each question.

THEN THERE'S YOU

Now you, unlike the guy next to you, have learned to use POE. You can spot obviously wrong answer choices from a mile away and typically get rid of at least two or three answer choices on every question. Therefore, even if you had to guess on every question on your test (which you never would) but first got rid of two or three answer choices each time, your proctor would be footing the bill for your first-semester books by the time the test was over. Imagine if you can eliminate three answer choices on every question, and then guess between the last two. You'd get about half the questions right. On a 25-question section, that's about 12 questions—or $12 from the proctor. And you'd only owe $3.25

for the 13 questions you got wrong. Do you see how using POE will increase your score? Every time you eliminate an answer choice, you increase your odds of picking the right answer, so you should always guess even if you can only cross off one choice.

THEN WHY AM I SKIPPING QUESTIONS?

Even though guessing increases your score, you should still skip some questions because, as we talked about earlier, skipping questions reduces time pressure and gives you a better chance of getting more questions right. Just remember the basic rule of thumb when it comes to skipping: *If you give a question your time, give it your best guess.* In other words, if you read a question that instantly feels too hard for you, skip it. But if you try a question, get rid of some answer choices, and then don't know what to do, take a smart guess. Solution #5: Work Smart, Guess Smart (Chapter 8) will give you lots of practice using POE and smart guessing.

HARD QUESTION STRATEGIES

Imagine that you just read the hardest question on the SAT and decided immediately that answer choice (B) was correct. Is your answer right? Probably not. Remember that all SAT questions have been tested on thousands of other test takers. The folks at ETS only designate a question as hard when they see that most testers are getting it wrong. In addition, when Aunt Thelma writes hard SAT questions, she includes answer choices designed to attract you—or, more accurately, distract you from the right answer choice. For example, let's watch how Thelma creates a hard analogy question, similar to one she created for us before:

23. MERITORIOUS : PRAISE :: (meritorious means deserving praise)
    (A)
    (B)
    (C)
    (D) reprehensible : censure (reprehensible means deserving censure)
    (E)

Thelma: Now, *since most students know the word praise but not meritorious, I'll put in a few answer choices that will make them think of the word praise.*

23. MERITORIOUS : PRAISE ::
    (A) captious : applause
    (B) kind : admiration
    (C)
    (D) reprehensible : censure
    (E)

There, those should distract them. All right, I'll just fill in answers for (C) and (E) and be done with this.

23. MERITORIOUS : PRAISE ::

(A) captious : applause
(B) kind : admiration
(C) questionable : retort
(D) reprehensible : censure
(E) incredible : ecstasy

But I Still Don't Know What Meritorious Means

To solve this analogy, you don't need to know exactly what meritorious means because you know how Thelma wrote the question. You know that this is one of the hardest questions on the test. Even if you can't think of the definition of meritorious, you know it has something to do with praise. Since this is a very hard question, (B) is a suspect answer, since "kind" and "admiration" are relatively easy words and "admiration" makes you think of "praise." You can cross choice (B) off immediately. What about the others? "Applause" in (A) also makes you think of "praise" and so is also unlikely to be right. Choices (C) and (E) don't have good defining relationships (more on that in the verbal chapter), so your smartest guess—and the right answer—is (D).

Stretch Your Vocabulary

Notice that the word "meritorious" in Aunt Thelma's hard example has the root "merit." You probably know what merit means, or at least you know that it's a good thing (merit awards, merit badges, etc). Therefore, you know that meritorious probably means something good that should be praised. This type of knowledge is often enough to get you to the right answer on the SAT.

Looks to Me Like You Know the Test Already

You just guessed this answer correctly without knowing the given words. How? You are beginning to know the test. You knew it was a hard question, and you know how hard questions are written. You used POE because you know that all but one of the answer choices on every SAT question are wrong. And you took a smart guess because you know that smart guessing will increase your score. Congratulations! I think you've got Solution #1 pretty well under your belt. Before we wrap up, though, I want you to meet a friend. . . .

BLOGGS, JANE BLOGGS

Meet Jane Bloggs. She is the average female test taker—she's not brilliant, she's not stupid, she's just average. And unlike you, she doesn't know the SAT. She's never heard of Order of Difficulty or Process of Elimination. Jane gets all the easy questions on the test right. She gets about half of the medium questions right, too. However, Jane gets all the hard questions wrong. Why? Because she always falls for the trap answer choices. On MERITORIOUS : PRAISE, she would definitely have picked one of Thelma's distractors.

ELIMINATE JANE ANSWERS

Would you want to take a test with Jane? Absolutely, because you would know that, on all the hard questions, what Jane thinks is right is usually wrong. So on hard SAT problems, simply consider what answers Jane might pick—and then cross off those choices. Try getting rid of the Jane Bloggs answers on the following question:

22. (SOME WORD YOU DON'T KNOW) : LANGUAGE ::

    (A) rhetoric : speech
    (B) syllogism : grammar
    (C) innovation : technology
    (D) iconography : art
    (E) epistemology : philosophy

First of all, you don't know one of the given words. You will need to guess on this question, but you can first use Jane to get rid of distracter answer choices. Remember that this is a hard question. What would Jane pick? (A) because of the word "speech," or (B), because of the word "grammar." Without doing any work, you know that these choices are probably wrong. If the obvious answer were right, this wouldn't be a hard question. So you can now guess among the remaining choices and move on. By knowing what the average Jane would do on hard questions, you know exactly what not to do, which means you can eliminate wrong answers. And if you eliminate even one answer choice, what should you do? Guess!

Now that you know the SAT, you're ready to move on to specific techniques for math and verbal questions. Turn to either Chapter 5: Do the Math or Chapter 6: Get Verbal to continue to close the gender gap.

Chapter 5
DO THE MATH

Homework

Before you read this chapter, complete:

Chapter 4 and at least:
Chapter 5 or 6

Solution #2: Do the Math

To close the gender gap in math, you must learn to do *SAT math*; and SAT math is not necessarily what you think it is. Even though the SAT is a test administered to high school juniors and seniors, the current SAT Math section tests mathematical concepts you learned either in freshman year or earlier. Therefore, some of what you need to do to prepare for the SAT Math section is review concepts that you haven't studied for a long time. In addition, There are several highly effective techniques you can use to solve SAT math problems quickly and easily.

As I mentioned in the first part of the book, the SAT rewards some test-taking behaviors that are not typically rewarded in school—things like taking shortcuts when you can, estimating instead of doing calculations, and Plugging In numbers instead of writing equations. While these may not be the ways in which most of us girls would choose to approach SAT math, we're smart enough to know that if we want to do well on the Math portion of the SAT, we'd better start doing SAT math.

This chapter will teach you what you need to know to do SAT math. Specifically, this chapter will teach you how to

- quickly and systematically solve arithmetic problems, such as averages, ratios, and percentages
- take on word problems one piece at a time
- solve most SAT algebra problems without ever writing an equation
- use Jane Bloggs to help you get rid of trap answer choices
- beat SAT geometry by learning how to play the geometry game
- solve quant comps and grid-ins quickly and accurately

AND IF I DON'T REMEMBER?

This chapter is designed to teach the math concepts and techniques that will be most helpful to girls taking the SAT. However, there may be other areas of SAT math that you need to review and other SAT techniques that could help you. For a complete review of all those arithmetic, algebra, and geometry concepts you don't remember, I strongly recommend that you work through The Princeton Review's *Cracking the SAT.*

A WORD ABOUT CALCULATORS

As you probably know, you are allowed to bring a calculator to the SAT. And, if at all possible, you should bring one. Calculators can save you time and effort. However, calculators can also become a crutch. On the SAT, it's more important that you understand a problem and know the kind of answer you should get before you start punching numbers into a calculator. You are the one taking the test, not your calculator. Your calculator won't recognize a trap answer, and it won't know how to use POE. Think first, and then use your calculator to make your life easier.

ARITHMETIC

WAY BACK WHEN

Do you remember when you didn't know how to do algebra? When math class consisted of arithmetic concepts such as fractions and long division? Once you learned algebra, you never went back to doing only arithmetic—you would use some arithmetic concepts to solve problems, of course, but by then these concepts were so ingrained that you rarely thought about what you were doing.

Well, way back when math was only arithmetic, you learned some other arithmetic concepts that did not necessarily become second nature, primarily because they aren't required all that often in more complex math. Some of these concepts—averages, percentages, and ratios—are tested repeatedly on the SAT. And although none of these concepts is unfamiliar to you, SAT-style averages, percentages, and ratios are a bit different from what you may have learned in middle school.

AVERAGES

Now, I know you're thinking, "Come on, I know how to find an average—just add up the numbers and then divide by how many numbers there are. What's hard about that?" Nothing. And if that were all ETS could think to do with averages, then they wouldn't bother to put them on the SAT. But SAT averages typically require a lot more than just adding up a column of numbers. To see what I mean, let's take a look at an example.

16. If the average (arithmetic mean) of four distinct positive integers is 11, what is the greatest possible value of any one of the integers?

(A) 35
(B) 38
(C) 40
(D) 41
(E) 44

Requires more than a little adding, huh? No worries. Here's how to do it: First, the term *arithmetic mean* that appears in parentheses is simply another way of saying average, so cross it out (see the Mean, Median, and Mode box for a quick review of the other types of terms you may encounter). Next, you need to decipher exactly what the question is asking. *Distinct* means different—in other words, none of the four numbers can be the same. *Positive*, as you probably know, means greater than zero. And *integers* are numbers other than fractions or decimals (they can be positive or negative). So, if you translate the first part of the question, you get, "If you add up four different positive numbers (not fractions or decimals) and then divide by four, you get eleven."

Mean, Median, and Mode

Mean or arithmetic mean—the kind of average you are used to (add up numbers and divide by the number of numbers).

Median—the middle number when numbers are arranged from least to greatest (like the median in the middle of the road). In the set {2 3 4 5 6}, the median number is 4. If there's an even number of numbers in the set, such as in the set {2 3 4 5}, then the median is the average of the two middle numbers. In this case, add 3 and 4, and then divide by 2. The median of the set {2 3 4 5} is 3.5.

Mode—the number that appears most frequently in a set. In the set {2, 3, 3, 4, 5}, the mode is 3.

THE AVERAGE PIE

Now, what does the *question* part of the question mean? In short, it's asking this: How big can the biggest of those four numbers be? How can you figure this out?

By using an Average Pie. There are three critical pieces to every average: the total (of the given numbers), the number of numbers you are given (in this case, four), and the average of those numbers (in this case, eleven). If you are given any two of those pieces of information in an average problem, you can use the average pie to find the third piece.

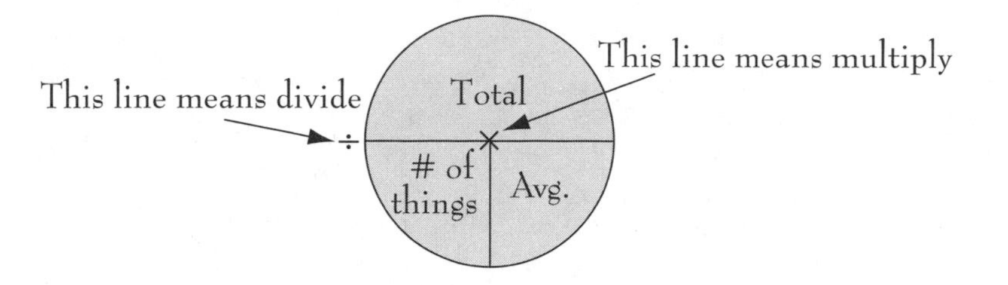

Since you have the number of numbers (4) and the average of those numbers (11), all you need to do is multiply them to get your total (which is 44). You are merely doing the opposite of what you would have done to get the average if you had been given the four numbers themselves (if you were given the numbers, you would have added them up and divided by four). Your Average Pie now looks like this:

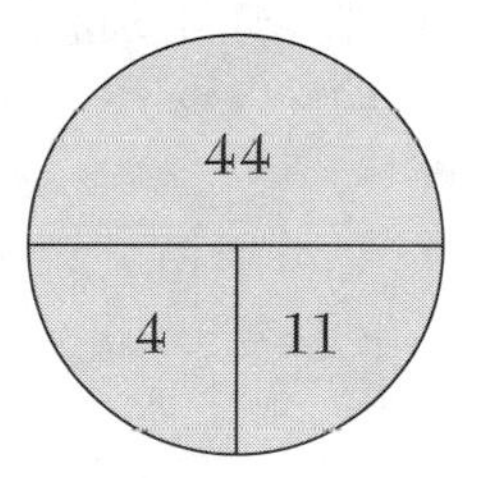

And How Does This Help?

Of course, finding the total doesn't answer the question—you need to figure out how big the biggest number can be, not what the total of the four numbers is—but you do need to first find the total in order to get the answer. You know that if you added together the four different numbers, your total would be 44. How can you make one of those numbers as big as possible? By making the other three numbers as small as possible. Let's say three of the numbers are 1, 2, and 3 (remember they have to be positive and different, so you cannot make them 1, 1, and 1). Then you would have: $1 + 2 + 3 + \text{something} = 44$. Now solve for the something: $44 - 6 = 38$. The biggest that fourth number can be is 38. Your answer is (B).

Aha. . .

Did you notice the trap answers that Thelma put in for you? (E) 44 is waiting for you in case you don't know what to do after multiplying 4 times 11. (D) 41 is there in case you figure out that you can make one number big by making the others small, but forget that the four numbers need to be distinct. But by using the Average Pie and your test smarts, you can easily and accurately solve this moderately difficult problem.

LET'S DO IT AGAIN

Try using the Average Pie to solve another problem:

Sales in May		
	Number Sold	Average Weight per Parrot (in pounds)
Red Parrots	5	2
Blue Parrots	4	3

12. The chart above shows the number of red and blue parrots Toby sold in May and the average weight of each type of bird sold. If Toby sold no other parrots, what was the average (arithmetic mean) weight ~~in pounds~~ of a parrot that Toby sold ~~in May?~~

(A) 2

(B) $2\frac{4}{9}$

(C) $2\frac{1}{2}$

(D) 5

(E) 9

First, let's take apart the word problem. The first sentence is merely a description of the chart, so you can basically ignore it. The beginning of the next sentence, "If Toby sold no other parrots," means the problem is only about the birds in the chart, so you can ignore that clause, too. Now for the important stuff: "What was the average (arithmetic mean) weight in pounds of a parrot that Toby sold in May?" First, double-check to see that the chart is giving the weight in pounds. It is, so cross that off; plus cross off the "in May," because there are no other months to consider. Now your question simply says, "What was the average weight of a parrot that Toby sold?" Get ready, get set, Average Pie. Draw one and label it to remind yourself of what goes where. Next, you need to draw an Average Pie for the red parrots and an Average Pie for the blue parrots.

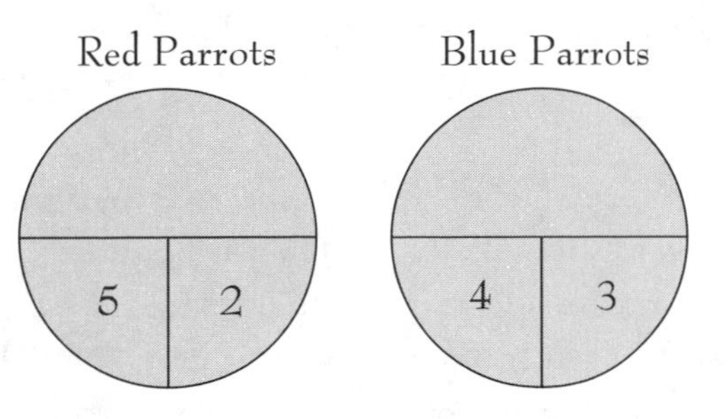

Now find the total weights for both the red and blue parrots by multiplying your number by your average in each pie. Fill in the totals above.

Now What?

The question wants to know the average weight of one parrot. Add together your totals to get the total weight of all the birds, and then divide that sum by the total number of birds. The total weight of the red parrots is 10 lbs., and the total weight of the blue parrots is 12 lbs. $10 + 12 = 22$. The total number is birds is 9. $22 \div 9$ birds $= 2\frac{4}{9}$. The answer is (B).

Did I Have to Do All That?

On the parrot problem, you may be wondering, "Couldn't I just have added together the average weight column and divided by two?" Try it. $2 + 3 = 5$. $5 \div 2 = 2\frac{1}{2}$. Not the same answer, but $2\frac{1}{2}$ is an answer choice. Thelma put that answer there just in case you made that mistake. Use your Average Pie (or pies, as the case may be) and you'll avoid getting caught in Thelma's traps.

Ratios

Who Wants Pizza?

Another arithmetic concept that doesn't get much attention in high school but does show up on the SAT is that of ratios. And ratios are actually something you use in real life fairly regularly. For example, every time you and a bunch of friends order pizza, you need to figure out how many pies to get. By counting on each person to eat 2 slices, you set up a ratio: 2 slices of pizza for every 1 person, or a ratio of 2:1. If you're ordering pizza with 5 friends, you know you'll need a total of 10 slices, and since each pie only has 8 slices, you'll need to order two pies. Using the same ratio of 2 slices for every 1 person, you could easily answer questions like, "How many people can you feed with one 8-slice pizza?" and "If you ordered two pies of 8 slices each to feed 5 people, how many additional people could you feed?"

Of course, the ratios on the SAT are not quite so simple. Instead of giving you the ratio of slices to people, for example, the SAT would give you something like this: "If each person at a party ate 2 plain slices for every 1 mushroom slice, and 36 total slices were consumed, how many mushroom slices were eaten?" Hmmm...you still have a ratio of 2: 1, but those numbers represent only a part of what is going on. How do you get from the ratio of 2 plain to 1 mushroom to 36 total slices and back? Enter the Ratio Box.

THE RATIO BOX

A ratio is not the same as a number. A ratio tells you the relationship between groups of things. To get from ratios to actual numbers, you must first find the whole or total. Let's try the pizza-party example from above :

	Plain	Mushroom	Total Slices
Ratio	2	1	
Multiply By			
Actual Number			36

To draw a Ratio Box, you need to draw a box with one column for each part of the ratio, plus an additional column for the total. You must also draw three rows: one for the ratio that you are given, one entitled Multiply By, and one for the actual number.

Once you draw your Ratio Box, fill in what you have been given. In the pizza-party example, you are told that each person ate 2 plain slices for every 1 mushroom slice. Under the appropriate columns, enter "2" and "1." You are also told that a total of 36 actual slices was consumed at the party—this is an actual number, so it goes in the bottom row under the Total Slices column.

WHAT HAPPENS NEXT?

To solve every ratio, you must first get a ratio total. In our example, you have a ratio of 2 plain slices to 1 mushroom slice, for a total of 3 slices. Write a "3" in the Total Slices column. How do you get from 3 total slices to 36 total slices? Multiply 3 by 12. And if you multiply any part of a ratio by something, you must multiply *every* part of the ratio by the same thing. In this case, write the number "12" in all three rows of the Multiply By column. Then, do what it says: Multiply each number in your ratio by 12.

Your Ratio Box now looks like this:

	Plain	Mushroom	Total Slices
Ratio	2	1	3
Multiply By	× 12	× 12	× 12
Actual Number	24	12	36

You now know that 24 actual plain slices were consumed, and 12 actual mushroom slices were consumed at the party, for a total of 36 slices (when you add across the columns of the numbers row, they should equal the actual number total).

How About Another Party?

Now, what if you were told that 50 plain slices were consumed at the party? Draw a new Ratio Box, fill in the ratio and ratio total, and then fill in the new actual number:

	Plain	Mushroom	Total Slices
Ratio	2	1	3
Multiply By			
Actual Number	50		

How do you go from 2 to 50? Multiply by 25.

	Plain	Mushroom	Total Slices
Ratio	2	1	3
Multiply By	× 25	× 25	× 25
Actual Number	50	25	75

How many total slices were consumed? How many mushroom slices? No matter what you are given, or what you are asked, repeat the same steps with the Ratio Box and you will get the information you need.

Does It Work on the SAT?

Let's try using the Ratio Box on an SAT problem:

10. A bakery uses a special flour mixture that contains corn, wheat, and rye in the ratio of 3:5:2. If a bag of the mixture contains 5 pounds of rye, how many pounds of wheat does it contain?

(A) 2
(B) 5
(C) 7.5
(D) 10
(E) 12.5

First, draw a Ratio Box with a column for each part of the ratio plus a total column. Enter the ratio numbers you are given, and then add them to determine your total.

	Corn	Wheat	Rye	Total
Ratio	3	5	2	10
Multiply By				
Actual Number				

Next, the problem says that the bag contains 5 actual pounds of rye—a real number, as opposed to a ratio number. Put a "5" in the Actual Number row of the Rye column. How do you get from 2 (ratio rye) to 5 (actual rye)? Multiply by 2.5. But if you multiply any part of a ratio by something, you must multiply every part of the ratio by the same thing. Your Ratio Box should now look like this:

	Corn	Wheat	Rye	Total
Ratio	3	5	2	10
Multiply By	× 2.5	× 2.5	× 2.5	× 2.5
Actual Number			5	

Now read the question part of the question. Since the question wants to know how many pounds of wheat there are, only do the math for the "wheat" column. Your Ratio Box now looks like this:

	Corn	Wheat	Rye	Total
Ratio	3	5	2	10
Multiply By	× 2.5	× 2.5	× 2.5	× 2.5
Actual Number		12.5	5	

How many pounds of wheat does it contain? 12.5—answer choice (E).

You get the idea. When confronted with a ratio problem, remember the Ratio Box and the difference between ratios and actual numbers. Also, when you are given a ratio, always think, "What's the total?" Finally, remember this rule: If you multiply any part of a ratio by a number, you must multiply every part of the ratio by that number.

PERCENTS

You will also need to be savvy in your ability to take percentages of numbers, particularly as part of a word problem. I'm sure you know that percent means "out of 100," and can do simple percents in your head. However, convoluted word problems sometimes make it hard to tell what you need to take the percentage of. Look at the following example:

7. Roberta has a collection of 80 CDs. If 40 percent of her CDs are classic rock and the rest are alternative, how many alternative CDs does she have?

    (A) 32
    (B) 40
    (C) 42
    (D) 48
    (E) 50

TRANSLATING PERCENTAGES

The first thing you need to do with any percentage word problem is to translate the problem from words into math. Use this handy-dandy translation guide to help you:

Words	Math
what	x, y, z (or letter of your choice)
what percent	$\frac{x}{100}$
of	$\times$
is, are, was, were	$=$

Let's translate the above problem: First, Roberta has 80 CDs.

Words: Roberta has 80 CDs.
If 40 percent of her CDs are classic rock . . .

Translate: $\frac{40}{100} \times 80 =$

Now cancel a few zeros (remember this?) and multiply:

$$\frac{4\not{0}}{10\not{0}} \times 8\not{0} = 32$$

How many alternative CDs does she have? Subtract 32 from 80 and you have answer choice (D).

Percents Aren't the Only Things You Can Translate

You can translate almost any word problem into a math problem. For example:

Maria needs to read half a 100-page book over the weekend (translation: $\frac{1}{2} \times 100 = 50$). If she reads one-fifth of the assigned pages on Friday night (translation: $\frac{1}{5} \times 50 = 10$), and one-fourth of the remaining pages on Saturday (translation: $\frac{1}{4} \times 40$ remaining pages $= 10$), how many pages does she need to read on Sunday? She has 30 pages left to read.

But Couldn't I Have...

There is a slightly faster way to solve the above problem: by actually beginning your work while you are pulling apart the word problem. For example, you could have read it this way: "If 40 percent of her CDs are classic rock, and the rest—*60%*—are alternative... ." Once you read the question part of the question, "How many alternative CDs does she have?" you can immediately take 60% of 80 CDs.

Translate: $\frac{6\not{0}}{10\not{0}} \times 8\not{0} = 48$

Which Way Is Right?

Which way should you solve this percentage problem? Should you push yourself to see the 60 percent from the start, or should you simply work with the numbers you are given? It really doesn't matter. Sometimes you'll see the 60 percent, and other times you won't, and either way is right. Your goal is to be so comfortable with percentages and translating word problems that you can solve each problem quickly and accurately. Try the example on the following page by translating from words to math.

15. A total of 60 beverages were sold at a school basketball game, some of which were diet and some of which were regular. If 40 percent of the first 30 sold were diet, 20 percent of the next 20 sold were diet, and 80 percent of the last 10 sold were diet, what percent of the total number of beverages sold was diet?

(A) 30

(B) $33\frac{1}{3}$

(C) 40

(D) $46\frac{2}{3}$

(E) 60

Before you can translate the question part of the question, you first need to translate each piece of this word problem to determine how many diet beverages were sold. Let's do it:

1. *words:* 40 percent of the first 30 sold were diet

   translate: $\frac{40}{100} \times 30 = \frac{4\not{0}}{1\not{0}\not{0}} \times 3\not{0} = 12$

2. *words:* 20 percent of the next 20 sold were diet

   translate: $\frac{20}{100} \times 20 = \frac{4\not{0}}{1\not{0}\not{0}} \times 2\not{0} = 4$

3. *words:* 80 percent of the last 10 sold were diet

   translate: $\frac{80}{100} \times 10 = \frac{8\not{0}}{1\not{0}\not{0}} \times 1\not{0} = 8$

Total number of diet beverages sold = 24

Now you can translate the question part of the question:

words: what percent of the total number of beverages sold were diet?

translate: $\frac{x}{100} \times 60 = 24$

calculate: $\frac{x}{10\not{0}} \times 6\not{0} = 24$

$\frac{6x}{10} = 24$

$6x = 240$

$x = \frac{240}{6}$

$x = 40$

answer: (C) 40

WORD PROBLEMS, PIECE BY PIECE

As you can see from the percentage word problem you just did, the key to solving word problems is to break them down into manageable pieces. To solve the above problem, you had to first solve each piece of the word problem before you could attempt to answer the question. Breaking down each word problem will allow you to solve it methodically, accurately, and rapidly. Look at an example:

15. Joline registered for four online publications that cost $13.90, $15.00, $22.00, and $17.90 per year, respectively. If she made an initial down payment of one-half of the total amount, and paid the rest in 4 equal monthly payments, how much was each of the 4 monthly payments?

    (A) $8.60
    (B) $9.20
    (C) $9.45
    (D) $17.20
    (E) $34.40

If your eyes begin to glaze over just from reading the problem, don't worry. It's hard to solve complex word problems all at once. However, it's easy to solve them when you do them One Piece at a Time. Let's take the first part only:

> Joline registered for four online publications that cost $13.90, $15.00, $22.00, and $17.90 per year, respectively. STOP!

First of all, you need to figure out what the total amount was. Add up the costs:

13.90
15.00
22.00
17.90
68.80 (good place to use a calculator)

> If she made an initial down payment of one-half of the total amount, STOP!

what's the down payment? Half of 68.80, or 34.40. So she has $34.40 left to pay. Go on:

> . . . and paid the rest in 4 equal monthly payments, how much was each of the 4 monthly payments?

"The rest" is $34.40. Divide 34.40 by 4 (use the calculator). You get $8.60. The answer is (A).

That's Just Stupid!

If you read the "Joline" problem and thought, "Who would bother to make four monthly magazine payments of $8 and change when you could just put the whole thing on a credit card?" then you were getting too caught up in the story. Reflecting on the absurdity of the scenarios can be good for comic relief during the test, but don't let it distract you from what you need to do.

ONE PIECE AT A TIME

Did solving that word problem One Piece at a Time make it more manageable for you? Let's try another:

18. Reading at a constant rate, it takes Aisha 7 hours to read 280 pages of her textbook. If Hanorah reads at twice this rate, how many <u>minutes</u> would it take Hanorah to read a textbook that contained 100 pages?

    (A) 60
    (B) 75
    (C) 90
    (D) 150
    (E) 300

Let's do the problem One Piece at a Time. The first part of the first sentence is necessary to know but won't be required in actually working through the problem, so cross it off. Let's start with the next part:

It takes Aisha 7 hours to read 280 pages of her textbook. 

That means she reads how many pages per hour? 40. Going on:

If Hanorah reads at twice this rate, STOP!

How many pages does Hanorah read per hour? Twice as many, or 80.
Next:

How many minutes would it take Hanorah to read a textbook that contained 100 pages?

She will read 80 pages in 1 hour (60 minutes), so it will take her a little bit longer than an hour to read 100 pages. Using just this information, let's use Process of Elimination (POE) to get rid of some answer choices. Which answer choices can you cross off?

~~(A)~~ 60
(B) 75
(C) 90
~~(D)~~ 150
~~(E)~~ 300

You should have crossed off (A), since we know it will take Hanorah longer than an hour, and (D) and (E) since it won't take her that long. You've gotten it down to two answer choices and have done hardly any math! If you had no idea how to finish this problem, you could take a very smart guess at this point.

Let's actually do the rest of the problem. Hanorah has 20 pages to go and reads 80 pages per hour. 20 is what percent of 80? (Translate if you need to.) 25% or $\frac{1}{4}$. How much does $\frac{1}{4}$ of an hour equal? 15 minutes. The answer? (B) 75 minutes.

ALGEBRA

PLUG IN THE ANSWERS (PITA)

Let's look at another word problem:

11. A woman made 5 payments on a loan with each payment being twice the amount of the preceding one. If the total of all 5 payments was $465, how much was the first payment?

    (A) $5
    (B) $15
    (C) $31
    (D) $93
    (E) $155

Upon first read, this word problem may not seem all that manageable, even piece by piece. However, notice what the question part of the question asks: "How much was the first payment?" The first payment was, according to the answer choices, $5, $15, $31, $93, or $155. Now, you could set up a slightly messy equation and hope that you don't make an error in calculation as you try to figure out her first payment, or you could solve this problem the SAT-smart way—by Plugging In The Answers. Let's try it. When you Plug In The Answers (PITA) to solve a question, begin with answer choice (C). If you get an answer that is too small, cross it off, plus cross off the answer choices that are smaller. If you get one that is too big, cross it off, plus the answer choices that are bigger.

Answer choice (C) is $31. If her first payment was $31, and each payment was twice as much as the previous payment, her five payments would look like this:

$31
$62
$124
$248
$496

You don't need to add up these numbers to see that the total would be way more than $465 (the total she actually paid according to the problem). Cross off (C), plus (D) and (E) since they are bigger still. Now let's try (B):

$15
$30
$60
$120
<u>$240</u>
$465

Was the total of all five payments $465? Yes. The answer is (B).

That's Why They're There

On the above question, there is absolutely no reason not to try the answer choices. The question asks you for a specific number—the amount of the first payment. Thelma was nice enough to give you five answer choices, and one of them must be right, so you might as well use them instead of hoping to create the right equation, battling time constraints, and risking errors. Let's see how PITA can help make a difficult problem easier:

18. Out of a total of 154 games played, a ball team won 54 more games than it lost. If there were no ties, how many games did the team win?

(A) 94
(B) 98
(C) 100
(D) 102
(E) 104

What does the question part of the question ask? How many games did the team win? What's the SAT-smart way to solve this problem? PITA. Let's start by checking answer choice (C) 100.

The team played 154 games, and won 54 more games than it lost. If it won 100, 100 – 54 = 46. It lost 46 games. But 100 wins plus 46 losses is only 146 games, and that's not enough games. Cross off (C). Also, since the total number of games was too small, you know that you need a bigger number. Cross off (A) and (B) as well.

Let's try (D):

Won = 102 Lost (102 – 54) = 48

102 + 48 = 150, still too small. Then the answer must be (E).

Should you check (E)? If this were the real SAT, no. However, since I know it's bugging you, let's do it.

Won = 104 Lost (104 – 54) = 50 104 + 50 = 154. That's it!

Why Didn't Anyone Tell Me?

PITA is an excellent method for solving multiple-choice questions, and one that is used by lots of savvy test takers. In fact, many test takers realize that they can solve problems in this fashion without ever being told to do so—however, most female test takers shy away from Plugging In The Answers because "it feels like cheating." It's not cheating, and it's not wrong—it's an efficient way to ensure accuracy on a timed test like the SAT.

When to PITA

When a math problem ends with a question like, "How old is Bill?" or "How many pages are in the book?" it has only one possible answer. When you read a question like that and are given five numeric answer choices (typically arranged in either increasing or decreasing order), the easiest way to solve that question is to Plug In The Answers. Try the middle answer choice first—if that doesn't work, you will then usually know whether you need a bigger or smaller number, and can eliminate answer choices without even trying them. Try Plugging In The Answers on the following problem:

19. The Smiths are replacing an existing square fence with a new square fence that is 2 feet longer per side than the old fence. Once installed, the new fence will make the Smith's fenced-in yard 40 square feet larger than it was previously. What is the length, in feet, of one side of the original fence?

 (A) 4
 (B) 6
 (C) 8
 (D) 9
 (E) 10

Begin by drawing a square fence and labeling one side 8, which is answer choice (C). If each side of the original square fence is 8 feet, the area of that square is 8^2 or 64 (remember: area of a square = side squared, or side × side). The new fence is 2 feet longer per side, making each side 10 feet long. A 10 by 10–foot square has an area of 100 feet. Is 100 40 more feet than 64? No, it's only 36 more. The answer choice is too small. Cross off (C), plus (A) and (B) since they are smaller still. Trying (D), if the old fence has sides of 9 feet, the area of the yard is 81 square feet. The new fence is 2 feet longer per side, or 11 feet on each side. 11 times 11 is 121. Is 121 40 feet bigger than 81? Yup. The answer is (D).

This represents a problem that would be considered relatively difficult on the SAT. But by Plugging In The Answers, your solution is easy, efficient, and clearly right. To solve any problem that asks for a numeric answer (how long was the fence?) and has a number in each answer choice, plug in the answers.

PLUG IN YOUR OWN NUMBER

Let's try another problem:

17. If 100 equally priced tickets cost a total of d dollars, 5 of these tickets cost how many dollars?

    (A) $\frac{d}{20}$

    (B) $\frac{d}{5}$

    (C) $5d$

    (D) $\frac{5}{d}$

    (E) $\frac{20}{d}$

In this problem, the question part of the question says, "5 of these tickets cost how many dollars?" If there were numbers in the answer choices, you could Plug In The Answers to solve this problem. However, in this problem, Thelma has replaced one number with the letter d. Who ever heard of tickets that cost d dollars? Imagine your phone conversation with Ticketmaster:

> "That brings your total to d dollars for those 100 equally priced tickets. Will that be VISA or MasterCard?"

No one uses variables in everyday conversation, so thinking in terms of variables can be a bit confusing. Plus, when you aren't using real numbers, it's hard to know if you've made a mistake. How can you solve SAT word problems that have variables in them? By Plugging In your own numbers.

Make up a number for d. Say 100 equally priced tickets cost a total of 200 dollars, (d = 200). That means each ticket costs two bucks (must be a school play). Now, what does the question want to know? 5 of these tickets cost how many dollars? If each ticket costs $2, then 5 tickets cost $10. Your answer is $10.

Now, you're probably thinking, "Well, that's nice, but none of the answer choices say \$10." In fact, one of those answers does say \$10, when you plug in 200 for d. \$10 represents your target number—the actual answer to the problem when you plug in your own number. To find the answer choice that says \$10, plug in your number (200) for the d in each answer choice.

(A) $\frac{200}{20} = 10$

That was quick. Do you need to check the rest? Because we are working with variables, yes, but do it the smart way—plug in 200 for all the d's, but don't do the calculations unless you have to. Here's how:

(B) $\frac{200}{5}$ is bigger than 10

(C) 5×200 is way to big

(D) $\frac{5}{200}$ is a fraction

(E) $\frac{20}{200}$ is also a fraction

Was that problem hard? According to Thelma it was. By Plugging In, you made this last of the medium problems a whole lot easier. Let's try another:

19. If c is positive, what percent of $3c$ is 9?

(A) $\frac{c}{100}\%$

(B) $\frac{c}{3}\%$

(C) $\frac{9}{c}\%$

(D) 3%

(E) $\frac{300}{c}\%$

When you see variables in a problem, what do you do? Plug in your own number. What would be a smart, easy number to plug in for c? The question part of the question says, "what percent of $3c$ is 9?" Good thing you already know how to solve percentage problems. If you chose to make $c = 4$, what percent of (4×3) is 9? Translate: $\frac{x}{100} \times 12 = 9$. Solve for x and you get 75%. Your target number, then, is 75%. Plug in 4 for all the c's in the answer choices, and remember not to do more math than you need to.

(A) $\frac{4}{100}\%$ is way too small. Cross it off.

(B) $\frac{4}{3}\%$ is not 75%. Cross it off.

(C) $\frac{9}{4}\%$ is not 75%. Cross it off.

(D) 3% Cross it off right away. The answer must be (E).

(E) $\frac{300}{4}\% = 75\%$. That's your target number!

Do you see how Plugging In can make your life a whole lot easier?

NO VARIABLES, NO NUMBERS

Take a look at this next question:

> 22. One-fifth of the cars in a parking lot are red, and $\frac{1}{2}$ of the red cars are SUVs. If $\frac{1}{4}$ of the SUVs in the parking lot are red, then what percent of the cars in the lot are neither red nor SUVs?

In this question, you are being asked to take fractional parts of a certain number of cars, but you don't know how many cars there are in the first place. It is much easier to take a fraction of something then it is to take a fraction of nothing, so plug in your own number.

You want to plug in a number that will make your life easy. Look at the fractions you will need to work with and the fact that the question is asking for a percentage, then pick a number that will be easy to work with (like 100). Assuming there are 100 cars in the parking lot, do the problem one piece at a time:

> One-fifth of the cars in a parking lot are red 

$\frac{1}{5} \times 100 = 20$. There are 20 red cars in the lot. Go on:

> and $\frac{1}{2}$ of the red cars are SUVs. STOP!

$\frac{1}{2} \times 20 = 10$. There are 10 red SUVs, and 10 other red cars. Go on:

> If $\frac{1}{4}$ of the SUVs in the parking lot are red STOP!

Hmmm...We know we have 10 red SUVs. $10 = \frac{1}{4} \times$ what number? 40. There are 40 SUVs in the parking lot. Now for the question part of the question:

What percent of the cars in the lot are neither red nor SUVs?

There are 40 SUVs and 10 additional red cars that are not SUVs, for a total of 50 SUVs and/or red cars. That's 50 out of 100. That means there are 50 other cars, neither SUV nor red. In other words, half the cars are neither SUV nor red. The answer is 50 percent.

This problem is a tough one, and also happens to be a grid-in, so there are no answer choices to check. But Plugging In still made this grid-in problem much more doable. Whenever you encounter variables in a problem, plug in your own number.

JANE BLOGGS

Remember Jane, our average test taker? Jane gets easy questions right and does so-so on the medium questions, but gets virtually all the hard questions wrong. Let's say you and Jane are working together on the following problem:

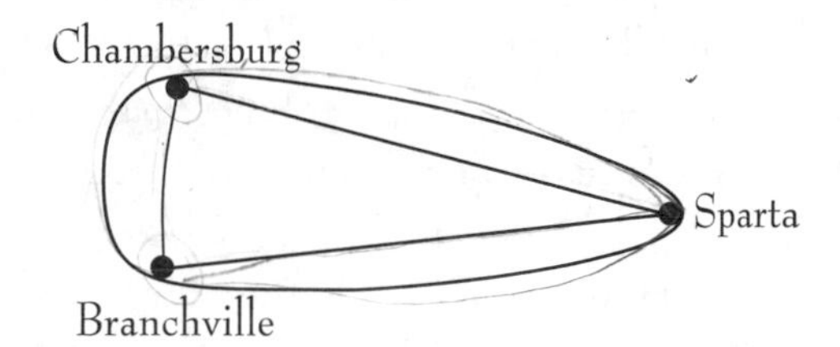

23. Gabrielle is traveling from Chambersburg to Branchville and back. The map above shows all the roads between Chambersburg, Sparta, and Branchville. How many different ways could she make the round trip, going through Sparta exactly once and not traveling any section of road more than once?

(A) 4
(B) 6
(C) 9
(D) 12
(E) 15

You: This is not math, it's Map-Reading 101.

Jane: It looks pretty easy to me—I know how to read a map.

You: Let's read the question one piece at a time to make sure we don't miss any important information. "Gabrielle is traveling from Chambersburg to Branchville and back"—let's circle those two towns on the map. How many different ways could she make the round trip, going through *Sparta only once* and *not traveling any section of road more than once*?

Jane: Isn't it two? I see two roads—the outside loop and the inside loop.

You: Look at the answer choices. The smallest choice is 4. Let's take a pencil and trace each possible route.

1 - *outside loop from C to S, outside loop S to B, outside loop back.*

2 – *outside loop C to S, inside road S to B, outside loop back.*

3 – *outside loop C to S, inside road S to B, inside road back.*

4 – *inside road C to S, outside loop S to B, outside loop back.*

5 – *inside road C to S, inside road S to B, outside loop back.*

6 – *inside road C to S, inside road S to B, inside road back.*

Jane: That's it. The answer must be 6—Oh, and there it is, letter (B). I love it when I find my answer!

You: But Jane, that was too easy. This is number 23 out of 25—it's one of the hardest questions on the test.

Jane: But you already figured out it was six. There aren't any other routes.

You: So what's the trick? Reread the question part of the question: "How many different ways could she make the round trip, going through Sparta exactly once...?" Wait... She doesn't have to go to Sparta first as long as she goes through Sparta once. She could do the whole loop in the opposite direction, going from Chambersburg to Branchville first, then coming home via Sparta. That would double the number of possible routes, so we'd have 12. Cross off (A), (B), and (C), since there are at least 12 routes. Are we missing any others? Well, if there are more than 12, the only other answer is 15—we're certainly not missing 3 routes, so the answer must be (D) 12.

Jane: Wow, I definitely would have gotten that wrong.

Thank You, Jane

Knowing what Jane will do on the hardest problems helps you know what *not* to do. Also, notice that that last problem wasn't even math, yet it would be considered one of the hardest problems on the entire SAT. And despite that, it was nothing more than a "tricky puzzle" (as one of the principals I interviewed likes to call them); a puzzle designed to see if you can identify the trick. Thanks to your newfound test know-how, and Jane's trustworthy mistakes, the hardest questions on the SAT are no longer hard.

GEOMETRY

What are you primarily asked to do on geometry questions? Why are girls not faring as well on SAT geometry questions as on other types of SAT math questions?

Girls may not be faring as well as boys on geometry problems because boys tend to have stronger visual-spatial skills. Or it may be because a lot of SAT geometry can be solved by using the kinds of shortcuts that girls tend not to take—like "guesstimating" the size of an angle or the length of the side of a square. Finally, the geometry you are used to doing now—proofs, theorems, etc.—is not the geometry that is tested on the SAT. Many girls have trouble with the geometry on the SAT because they cannot believe it is really testing such basic concepts as the area of a circle instead of sine and cosine.

Take a look at a problem to see what I mean:

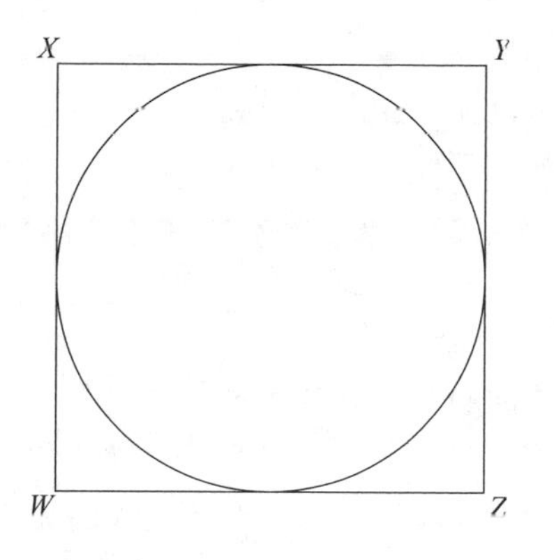

20. In the figure above, a circle is inscribed in square *WXYZ*. If the area of the circle is 400π, what is the area of *WXYZ*?

What do you need to know to solve this problem? Two things: how to get the area of a circle, and how to get the area of a square. Do you remember when you learned that stuff? It wasn't in high school. The SAT does include a table at the beginning of the math section with reminder formulas for these things, but a quick review is all you'll need. Let's do this problem:

Area of a circle equals πr^2. If the area of this circle is 400π, what is the radius? The square root of 400, or 20. If the radius (the line from the center of the circle to the outside of the circle) is 20, then the diameter is 40—and the diameter is the same length as one side of the square. How do you get the area of a square? Side × side or $40 \times 40 = 1600$. That's it.

All Shapes and Sizes

Circles

Area = πr^2 Circumference = $2\pi r$ or πd Degree measure = 360°

Rectangles

Area = length × width Perimeter = add all four sides

Inside angles total 360° (each angle = 90°)

Squares (rectangles with sides of equal length)

Area = side × side Perimeter = add all four sides

Inside angles total 360° (each angle = 90°)

Triangles

Area = $\frac{bh}{2}$ Perimeter = add all three sides

Inside angles total 180°

ARE YOU SURE?

Many girls also have a lot of trouble accepting that SAT diagrams are simply what they appear to be. When dealing with any SAT geometry problem, remember these basic rules:

1. **Unless otherwise stated, every picture is drawn to scale.** This rule means that you can guesstimate—eyeball it to see how big it looks—or even measure the size or length of figures on the SAT. For example, if you are told that one side of a rectangle measures 2, you can actually use the length of that line to "measure" the length of the other side of the rectangle. Even though you would never solve a problem this way in school, feel free to use this shortcut on SAT geometry problems.

2. **If a diagram says it is not drawn to scale, don't trust it.** If Thelma decides to draw a diagram that is not drawn to scale, she is doing so to trick you. Something about that diagram is misleading, so don't use it. Use the information in the problem to draw your own diagram instead.

3. **If there is no diagram, draw your own.** Likewise, if Thelma leaves the diagram out, she is hoping that you will try to solve the problem in your head. Don't fall for it—draw a picture to represent the problem, then solve the problem the smart way.

CAN YOU VISUALIZE IT?

First let's look at a geometry problem that has no picture:

15. Seven circles, each with radius 1.5 centimeters, are placed along a straight line with adjacent circles touching. What is the distance, in centimeters, between the center of the first circle and the center of the last circle?

    (A) 7
    (B) 10.5
    (C) 15
    (D) 18
    (E) 21

The first thing you need to do to solve this problem is draw a picture. The problem describes seven circles placed along a straight line with adjacent circles touching. Your picture would look something like this:

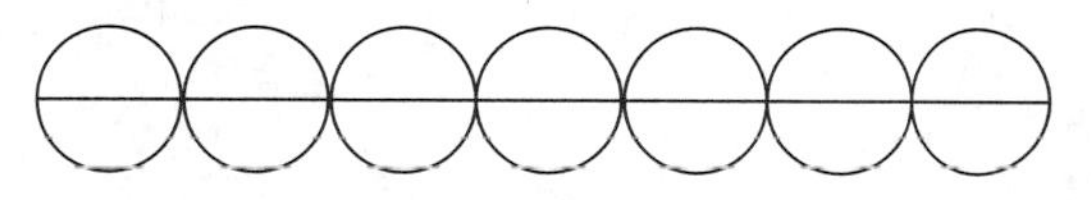

Now, each circle has a radius of 1.5. If the radius of a circle is 1.5, the diameter is twice that, or 3. Now, the question wants to know the distance from the center of the first circle to the center of the last circle. First let's figure out the distance between the first and last circles:

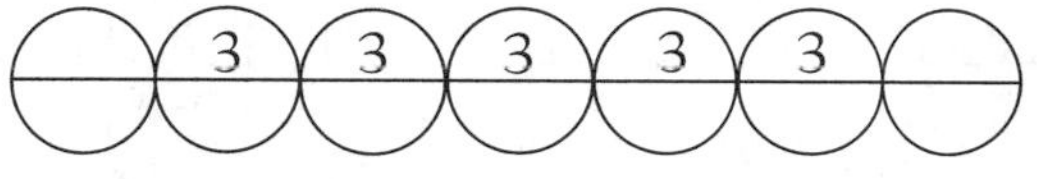

$5 \times 3 = 15$. You know your answer has to be bigger than 15, so what answer choices can you cross off? Now you need to add the distance of the radii of both the first and last circles: $1.5 + 1.5 = 3$. $15 + 3 = 18$. Your answer is (D). By drawing your own diagram, this question becomes easy to visualize and easy to do.

What a Picture!

Now let's try a few in which the diagram is provided. First look at this example:

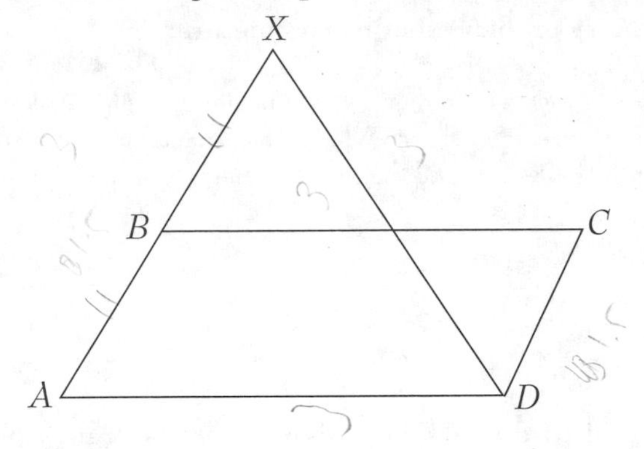

8. In the figure above, ΔAXD is equilateral and ABCD is a parallelogram. If B is the midpoint of AX and the perimeter of ΔAXD is 9, what is the perimeter of ABCD?

   (A) 15
   (B) 12
   (C) 9
   (D) 8
   (E) 6

Don't let the terminology or the diagram throw you. Remember that when a diagram is given in a geometry problem, most of the rest of the problem is merely a verbal description of the diagram. Take the problem apart a piece at a time, picking out any additional information the words provide, and crossing out the redundant stuff:

ΔAXD is equilateral...

Equilateral means all sides and all angles are equal. Since the inside angles of a triangle add up to 180° and there are three equal angles in this triangle, each angle is 60° ($180 \div 3 = 60$). Go on:

...and ABCD is a parallelogram. 

You can tell that from the picture, so cross this off (see the Parallelograms and More box for a quick review of parallelograms and angles). Go on:

If B is the midpoint (exact middle) of AX, and the perimeter of ΔAXD is 9...

"Perimeter" means the sum of the outside lines of a figure. If the perimeter of an equilateral triangle is 9, then each side equals 3 (because all three sides are equal). That means AX equals 3. If B is the midpoint of AX, line AB equals 1.5 and line BX equals 1.5. Label your diagram and then read the question part of the question:

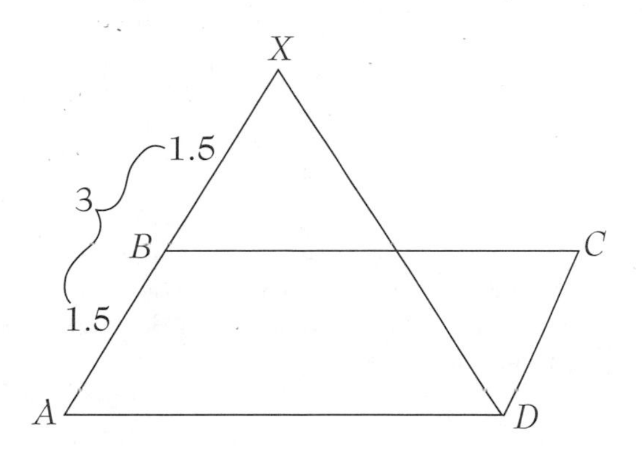

... what is the perimeter of ABCD?

You know that AB equals 1.5, which means CD equals 1.5 (parallelogram). You know that AD equals 3, which means BC equals 3. Add your outsides, and you're done. The answer is (C).

Parallelograms and More

As the name "parallelogram" implies, the opposite sides in any parallelogram are parallel. The inside angles add up to 360°. If you look at the information given for question 8, you can actually figure out the sizes of all the angles in the diagram. You know that angle A equals 60° (part of the equilateral triangle). In a parallelogram (and with any line that cuts two parallel lines), the small angles are equal to each other, the big angles are equal to each other, and a small angle plus a big angle equals 180°. Therefore, angle C equals 60°, and angles B and D each equal 120°.

DIDN'T THAT TAKE TOO LONG?

When you are first working with geometry, it may seem to take a long time to get to the answer. However, your goal in practice is to be able to efficiently fill in the important information in any diagram. Practice by doing a bunch of geometry problems and filling in everything you can figure out, not just what the question asks. Doing this will hone your geometry skills and your geometry confidence. On the test itself, however, you should just do what you need to solve the question—nothing more.

Let's try a slightly harder problem:

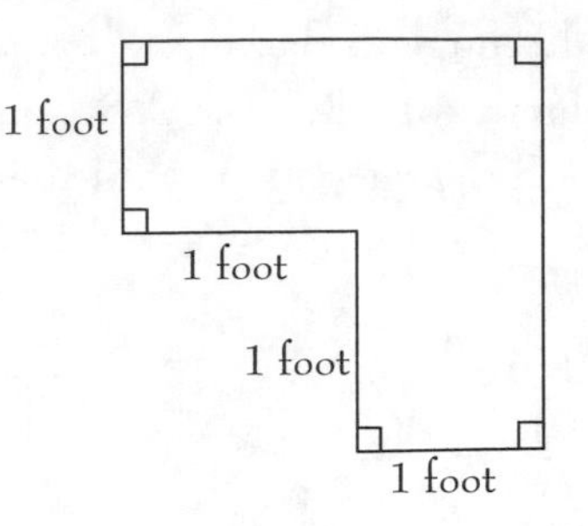

22. Bathrooms Beautiful is tiling a 15-foot by 10-foot bathroom with custom tiles that are the shape and dimensions shown above. Tiles come in boxes of 20. What is the minimum number of boxes of tiles Bathrooms Beautiful will need to purchase to complete the job?

    (A) 1
    (B) 2
    (C) 3
    (D) 4
    (E) 5

First let's work with the diagram. You have a funky-shaped tile and some of the sides are labeled. Can you see how this tile is merely a square with the bottom 25% missing? That means each of the long sides measures 2 feet (1 foot + 1 foot from the cut-out corner). Now, you know the bathroom can't be tiled without some finagling; if you just put the tiles down side by side, you'd have little square holes in the floor. What can you do to make a solid rectangular tile with dimensions that will conveniently divide into a 15 by 10-foot room (you didn't think the numbers were picked randomly, did you)? Lay one tile down as is, then flip the next one so that it interlocks with the first and looks something like this (draw it for yourself):

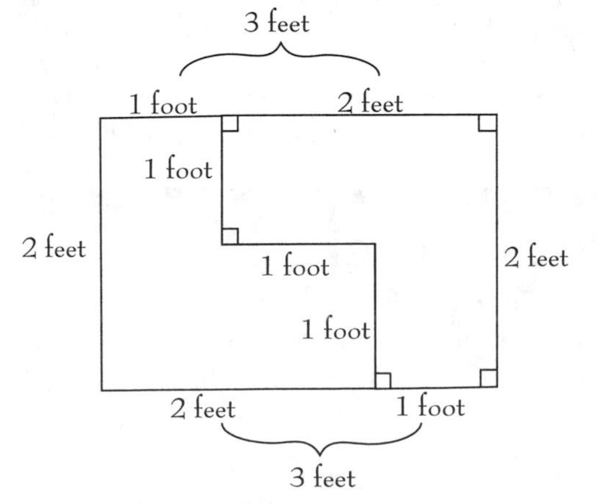

Now you have a rectangular double tile (created by putting together two tiles) with dimensions 3×2. That makes the area of the new double tile 6 (area = length × width). The area of the 15 by 10–foot room is 150. How many of these double tiles would it take to tile the floor? Divide the area of the room by the area of the double tile: $150 \div 6 = 25$. So you'd need 25 of the double tiles you created, or 50 of the original custom tiles. What does the question part of the question ask?

> What is the minimum number of boxes of tiles Bathrooms Beautiful needs to complete the job?

Tiles come in boxes of 20, and you need 50 tiles, so you need a minimum of 3 boxes—(C).

Whenever you encounter a geometry problem, draw what you need or use the diagram given to make the problem more concrete—more real. Then solve it like any other word problem, One Piece at a Time.

Now let's try Plugging In your own number on a geometry problem:

25. The length of rectangle S is 20 percent longer than the length of square R, and the width of rectangle S is 20 percent shorter than the width of square R. The area of rectangle S is

    (A) 20% greater than the area of square R
    (B) 4% greater than the area of square R
    (C) equal to the area of square R
    (D) 4% less than the area of square R
    (E) 20% less than the area of square R

What makes this problem a number 25? It's geometry with no diagram, no numbers, and a lengthy, convoluted explanation—that's all. The first thing you need to do to solve this problem is draw a diagram. Draw two rectangles, R and S. Then ask yourself: How can you make one side of S 20% longer than R, and the other side 20% shorter than R? By Plugging In real numbers, of course. Try making both the length and the width of R 10 (yes, it's okay—a square is still a rectangle). What is 20% of 10? 2. The length of S is 20% longer, so it's 12, because $10 + 2 = 12$. The width of S is 20% shorter, so it's 8, because $10 - 2 = 8$. Your diagram should look like this (don't worry, yours doesn't have to be drawn to scale):

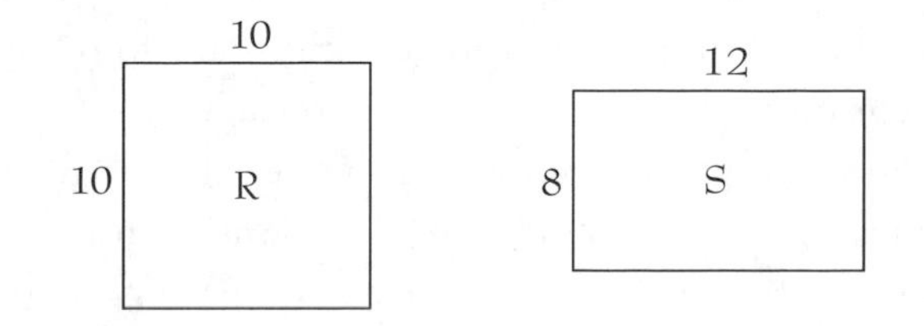

What Was the Question?

Now read the question part of the question. "The area of rectangle S is..." Figure it out—length × width, so 8 × 12 = 96. But look at the answer choices again:

(A) 20% greater than the area of square *R*
(B) 4% greater than the area of square *R*
(C) equal to the area of square *R*
(D) 4% less than the area of square *R*
(E) 20% less than the area of square *R*

They all compare the area of S to the area of R, so you need to find the area of R. 10 × 10 = 100, so the area is 100. Now, a smart look at the given answer choices should tell you that Jane is clearly leaning toward (C)—"you know, same increase as decrease must make them equal"—or (A) or (E) since she truly has no idea how to do this problem. So what's left? (B) the area of S is 4% greater than R, or (D) the area of S is 4% less than R. Now let's do the math. 96 (the area of S) is 4 less than 100 (the area of R), so the answer must be (D).

Was That Hard?

Did that seem hard to you? If so, that's okay. Even if it was a bit tricky, that problem was not nearly as hard as it seemed when you first read it. And notice how many of the techniques you combined—drawing it for yourself, Plugging In your own numbers, and relying on good old Jane—to make this hard problem less difficult.

QUANT COMP

Jane's Worst Nightmare

The Quantitative Comparison portion of the Math SAT (quant comp for short) is full of tricks and traps. It also is a section that clearly rewards taking that shortcut, girls. Luckily, it is also extremely coachable (maybe that's why they are getting rid of it in 2005). Once you know the rules of quant comp, I think you'll actually enjoy taking these shortcuts.

Always, Always

The directions for the quant comp portion of the SAT are long and confusing, so you won't want to read them on test day. Here's what you need to know: You are given two columns (A and B) and are supposed to decide whether the quantity (number, equation, etc.) in column A is bigger, smaller, or equal to the quantity in column B. If you pick A for your answer, that means that column A is always, always bigger than column B. If you pick B, that means that column B is always, always bigger than column A. If you pick C, that means that columns A and B are always, always equal. Answer choice D is for "Don't Know"—sometimes column A is bigger, sometimes B is bigger, etc.

Do not pick E—it is not an answer choice on quant comp.

Let's try a problem:

Notice first that the answer choices are not given, which makes using POE a little tricky. Therefore, for each question, jot down a quick "A B C D," because POE is critically important to getting quant comp problems right. Now, since there are variables in this question, how do we solve it? Plug in! Start with something easy like 2. If x is 2 (column A), x^2 is 4 (column B). Which column is bigger? B. Cross off A and C. By showing that column B is bigger even once, you have proven that column A is not always, always bigger, and that the two columns are not always, always equal.

Isn't It B?

Should you just go ahead and pick B as your answer? Not yet. First you must see if there are numbers you can use that might produce a different answer—a number that may act a little differently when squared, numbers like fractions, negatives, zero, or 1.

Let's try the number 1 in the above problem. If x is 1 (column A), x^2 is also 1 (column B). That means that columns A and B are equal. If the two columns are equal, the answer cannot be B because B is not always, always bigger (it also can't be A, but you already crossed off A). Cross off B. What are you left with? D for Don't Know. If you had plugged in a fraction between zero and one on this problem, you would have gotten column A as bigger (fractions get smaller when they are squared). As you can see, a little Plugging In will go a long way when it comes to quant comp.

DFONZ

When it comes to Plugging In on quant comp, you will typically need to do it twice—once with a nice, easy number, and then once with a weird number such as a Different-sized number (really big, or really small), Fraction, One, Negative, or Zero (DFONZ). Each time you go to plug in a weird number, size up the problem to see what kind of number might make a difference. For example, when you are squaring numbers, a negative number is good to try since a negative squared becomes positive.

SAY THAT AGAIN

Let's review how to solve quant comps:

1. Write "A B C D" next to every question.
2. Put in an easy, straightforward number for the variable.
3. If column A is bigger than column B, cross off answer choices B and C. If column B is bigger, cross off A and C. If they are equal, cross off A and B.
4. Solve the problem again, looking for the trick and trying DFONZ. Plug in at least twice, using as many of the DFONZ options as you need to ensure you've found the answer. If you get a different outcome when you use different kinds of numbers, the correct answer is D.

MEET THEIR DEMANDS FIRST

On many quant comps you will be given information, centered between the columns, that must be true. Therefore, if you are plugging in numbers, your numbers must first meet the requirements of the given information.

On the example we just did, you might be given something like this:

2.

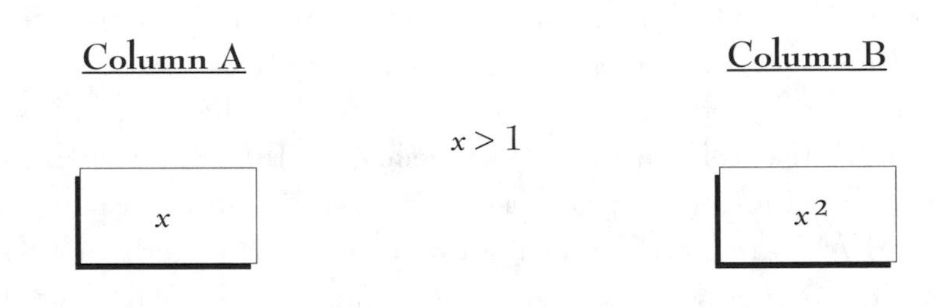

Because of the given information—that x must be greater than 1—Column B will always be bigger. (The only DFONZ number you can plug in is a different-sized number, which won't make a difference in this problem—plugging in 2, 20, 200, or 2000 will all make column B bigger, so the answer must be (B). What about this:

9.

Column A		Column B
	$0 < x < 1$	
x		x^2

Now the only number you can plug in for x is a fraction between 0 and 1. These fractions get smaller when they are squared; for example, $\frac{1}{2}$ squared is $\frac{1}{4}$. For this question, column A will always, always be bigger. Notice how the given information changes both the answer and the level of difficulty of the problem.

WHAT'S WRONG WITH THEIR NUMBER?

Look at this example:

11.

Column A	Column B

x, y, and z are positive
$x + y + z = 10$ and $x = y$

Why do you suppose Thelma put a 5 under column B? Remember, nothing on the SAT is random, so let's find out why. Make x equal to 5 and see what happens. If $x = 5$, then $y = 5$ too, since the given info says that $x = y$. $5 + 5 + z = 10$, but $5 + 5$ already equals 10. That would make $z = 0$. Is that okay? Not according to the given information—x, y, and z must all be positive, and zero is neither positive nor negative. So can x equal 5? No. Can x be bigger than 5? No, because then z would be negative (try it if you don't see it). x must always, always be smaller than 5, so the answer is B—column B is always, always bigger. Knowing that nothing is random on the SAT can give you the heads up you need to do the right thing with the problem—in this case, to cut right to the chase and plug in the number Thelma put in column B just for you.

FOR JANE'S SAKE

Let's try one more to see how Jane gets caught in quant comps:

13.

First, since there are no variables, you know there is a definitive answer to this question, so cross off D. What answer is Jane leaning toward? She sees the numbers 30 and 60, and immediately assumes that the larger number will have more prime factors, so she's going for B. But this is a difficult question, number 13 out of 15 quant comp questions. It's very unlikely that the answer would be so obvious. Cross off B. If you don't know what else to do, you have a fifty-fifty shot of guessing the question right. But let's do it.

First, get the factors of 30—you remember, the small numbers that you break big numbers down into (if you don't remember how to do this, you need to review your math!).

<u>30</u>

1 30

2 15

3 10

5 6

Now circle the distinct (different) prime (only divisible by 1 and itself) factors of 30, keeping in mind that 1 is not a prime number.

30

1 30

(2) 15

(3) 10

(5) 6

There are three. Now do the same for 60.

	60
1	60
(2)	30
(3)	20
4	15
(5)	12
6	10

Once again, there are three. The answer is C. By following your quant comp rules and knowing what not to do (thanks again, Jane), you just got one of the hardest quant comps on the test right.

GRID-INS

WHERE DID THE ANSWERS GO?

Try the following problem:

23. At a video rental store, the price to rent a DVD is twice the price to rent a video cassette. If 80 DVDs were rented out for a total of $480, and the combined income from DVDs and video cassette rentals was $600, how many video cassettes were rented?

You know by now that Plugging In The Answers is the way to go on questions that ask things like, "How many video cassettes were rented?" But wait...there are no answer choices to this problem! It's a grid-in, the kind of question in which you have to actually do the math and then "grid-in" your answer. Won't this be harder?

Not necessarily. In this example, you cannot PITA because there are no answer choices, but you can take this word problem apart One Piece at a Time to find your answer. Let's try it.

> The price to rent a DVD is twice the price to rent a video cassette. If 80 DVDs were rented out for a total of $480 STOP!

80 DVDs cost \$480. $480 \div 80 = 6$. So DVDs cost \$6 to rent, and videos cost \$3 (DVDs cost twice as much to rent). Go on:

...and the combined income from DVDs and video cassette rentals was \$600 

The combined income was \$600, \$480 of which was DVDs. That means the store made \$120 by renting videos. Videos cost \$3 each to rent. $120 \div 3 = 40$. What does the question part of the question ask? "How many video cassettes were rented?" You already figured out the answer: 40. Grid it in. This was considered one of the harder grid-in questions. Was it really hard? Hardly, because you took it One Piece at a Time. Don't let the absence of answers make you any less confident in your test-taking ability.

But How Do I Grid In?

Be sure to read through the instructions for the grid-in questions before test day, and to practice gridding in a few times. The basic rules of gridding in are:

- Before you grid in, always write your answer in the boxes at the top of the grid.
- Always place the first number in the far left column (be consistent and avoid confusion).
- After you've written in your answer, grid it in by darkening the corresponding numbers below.
- You can grid in fractions or decimals, but not mixed numbers.
- Fractions do not need to be reduced if they fit in the grid.
- If you grid in a decimal, include as many places of the decimal as fit in the grid. Do not include a zero before the decimal point.
- Some problems ask for a range and therefore have more than one correct answer. Grid in your favorite option.

Whew! That was a lot of math to learn. You've learned a lot of important SAT math concepts, plus some very powerful techniques. What do you need to do next? Practice. To practice math, work through a few tests in either *10 Real SATs* or *Cracking the SAT.* Go through a section by first identifying how to solve each problem. Then, go back and do sets of similar problems (all the PITA in a section, all the averages in a section, etc.) Once you feel comfortable with the techniques for each question type, start doing timed work in *Cracking the SAT* and *10 Real SATs.* (Use Chapter 7 as your guide to doing timed practice.)

And remember to do the math—SAT math.

Chapter 6
GET VERBAL

Solution #3: Get Verbal

There are many kinds of verbal skills—writing, grammar and language use, reading comprehension, etc. And there are many different ways to assess verbal skills. However, ETS tests just two verbal skills—vocabulary knowledge and reading comprehension. And it tests them in an artificial way—the method it uses to evaluate "critical reading" skills has very little to do with reading, and much of the vocabulary tested is, in the words of one of my colleagues, "just plain weird."

To do well on SAT Verbal, you need to get verbal in two ways: You need to understand what ETS means by "verbal," and you need to verbalize your answers (answer questions in your own words) before you get caught up in the answer choices. This chapter will teach you verbal skills á la ETS, by teaching you

- how to build your SAT vocabulary
- how to do sentence completions without ever testing an answer choice to see if it "sounds good"
- how to solve analogies whether or not you know the given words
- how to get critical reading questions right while only reading some of each passage

SAT Vocabulary

Would you classify your vocabulary as stellar, mediocre, or abysmal? Are SAT vocabulary words commonplace to you, or are they instead impenetrable and abstruse? Even if you have a decent vocabulary, you need to develop your *SAT vocabulary*.

The best way to beef up on SAT vocabulary words is to take the time to learn the vocabulary you encounter while you practice for the test. As you do verbal questions in a book like 10 Real SATs, you're bound to come across words you don't know. These are absolutely the best words for you to learn, because they are among the words most likely to appear on the test.

But I'm Busy

Now, when you're practicing for the SATs, you shouldn't stop every two seconds to pull out the dictionary. In fact, you should definitely not look up a word when you are in the middle of a verbal problem, because you won't be able to do that on test day. Instead, every time you come across a vocabulary word that you don't know, or even a word that you "sort of" know but aren't sure of, circle it. After you've completed the problem (or set of problems), take a vocabulary break. Create a "Vocabulary Stash" for yourself by writing down each word you circled. Look up the definitions of the words you stash, then try to remember them in your own words. If you need help, ask your mom, dad, or teacher to explain the word to you in a way that will "make it real."

Don't Just Stash 'Em

Writing down words and their definitions is a good start, but it's not enough. As your Vocabulary Stash grows, you need to use the words you've stashed in your everyday conversation or writing, or those words will fade from your memory. Set aside time to work on just vocab. Take your stash and try to write sentences with the words, or group similar words together. Pick a few and use them in conversation. The more you use the words, the more they will become a part of your life. And one good thing about learning SAT vocabulary is that these words will be useful to you during college and beyond.

Stretch Your Vocabulary

You know a lot more words than you think you do. Just because you can't spit out a dictionary definition of a word doesn't mean you don't know what it means. Even partial knowledge of a word is a useful thing on the SAT—as you'll soon see.

Be Resourceful

Of course, there are lots of other ways to learn vocabulary. The more you read, the more vocab you come across. As you read the paper, your favorite magazine, an assignment for school, or even some trashy novel, circle the words you don't know (since most of us don't want to stop in the middle of something to look up a word) and add them to your stash. Then treat each word like any other vocab word you need to learn—look it up, define it in your words, and use it. It's also helpful to go back to where you found the word and read it again in context once you know what it means.

There are also some good vocab-building books you can work through. Of course, Cracking the SAT has a great SAT vocab section. In addition, The Princeton Review also puts out the Word Smart and Illustrated Word Smart books to help you improve your vocabulary.

Mnemonics Are Goofy

Sometimes certain words just won't stick in your mind. For these words, try creating mnemonic devices—memory tricks or silly sentences that help you remember what a word means. For example, I can never remember exactly what the word *iconoclast* means. I always think it means the same thing as "icon" or symbol, but it actually means one who attacks popular ideas and traditions. So here's a mnemonic device for iconoclast:

That iconoclast likes to blast traditional icons.

Now, if I say this silly mnemonic device the next few times I see the word iconoclast, I probably won't forget this word again. If you were to use this mnemonic device or create your own device for the words you can't remember, you would be more likely to remember them when you need to—like on the SAT. For example:

14. ICONOCLAST : TRADITION ::

    (A) researcher : theory
    (B) conformist : expectation
    (C) anarchist : government
    (D) deceiver : law
    (E) officer : violence

What is an iconoclast? That iconoclast likes to blast traditional icons. An ICONOCLAST is someone against TRADITION. Now use this sentence to check each answer choice:

(A) Is a *researcher* someone against *theory*? No, so cross it off.

(B) Is a *conformist* someone against *expectations*? No, just the opposite. Cross it out.

(C) Is an *anarchist* someone against *government*? Yes. Keep it.

(D) Is a *deceiver* someone against the *law*? Not necessarily, it is simply one who is dishonest. If you are unsure, keep it.

(E) Is an *officer* someone against *violence*? No. Cross it off.

Your best answer choice is (C). Use mnemonic devices and any other method you know to learn as many SAT Vocab words as you can. The more SAT words you know, the easier the verbal section of the test will be.

SENTENCE COMPLETIONS

Sentence completions is the first type of question on both of the 30-minute Verbal sections. You'll be given either nine or ten sentences. Each sentence will contain one or two blanks. It is up to you to decide which answer choice word (or words) fits best in the blank (or blanks).

WHO COMPLETES THE SENTENCE?

How do you solve sentence completions? Many testers, before they learn how to approach this type of problem, use the "sounds good" method:

1. Since the region's soil has been barren for so many years, the locals must now ____ much of their food.

    (A) deliver
    (B) import
    (C) produce
    (D) develop
    (E) utilize

Hmmm...okay, let's try 'em. "...the locals must now <u>deliver</u> much of their food." Deliver...to where? No, I don't think that sounds right. How about (B): "...the locals must now <u>import</u> much of their food." I guess they could—doesn't say from where, but... Try (C): "...the locals must now <u>produce</u> much of their food." Well, that would be good—but it does say that the soil is barren. So it would be good if they could, but I don't know if that's the answer. Try (D): "...the locals must now <u>develop</u> much of their food." Well, that's sort of the same thing. It sounds possible. Try (E): "...the locals must now <u>utilize</u> much of their food." What, eat it? That's weird. I don't think so. So, it's either (B), (C), or (D). Now I'll use them again in the whole sentence:

"Since the region's soil has been barren for so many years, the locals must now <u>import</u> much of their food."

"Since the region's soil has been barren for so many years, the locals must now <u>produce</u> much of their food."

"Since the region's soil has been barren for so many years, the locals must now <u>develop</u> much of their food."

Well, they all sound okay, but since the soil has been barren for years, my guess is that producing or developing would be tough. I think the answer they want here is <u>import</u>. I'll guess (B).

As you can see, the "sounds good" method of evaluating sentence completions answer choices is pretty inefficient. On harder questions, it may actually lead you to wrong answers. Why? Because Thelma, our test writer, designed them to sound good. If you were to read every sentence completion five times and simply put each answer choice in the blank, most of the choices would *sound* just fine. But sounding good does not make an answer choice right. In fact, on the hardest sentence completions, the "sounds good" answer is invariably wrong (just ask Jane Bloggs). Instead of testing answer choices, then, you need a much more efficient way to get to the word Thelma chose as the right answer. First you need to know how she wrote the question.

SO THAT'S HOW THEY DO IT

When Thelma writes a sentence completion, she decides how hard the question needs to be, picks a topic, and then begins to create a sentence:

Thelma: Let's write an easy question first. I'll write about how some animal behaviors are innate—in fact, "innate" can be the right answer. Some animal behaviors are blank... immune to external factors... that's a good clue for the word innate. How about this:

1. Certain animal behaviors, such as mating practices, seem to be _____ , and therefore are immune to external factors such as climate changes, food supply, or the presence of other animals of the same species.

(A)
(B) innate
(C)
(D)
(E)

Thelma: That works. Now for the wrong answers. I'll make (A) "learned." What other words would sound good in this sentence? How about "intricate" and "specific"? Good. Now, one more. I guess "memorized" will work. Let's see:

1. Certain animal behaviors, such as mating practices, seem to be _____, and therefore are immune to external factors such as climate changes, food supply, or the presence of other animals of the same species.

(A) learned
(B) innate
(C) intricate
(D) specific
(E) memorized

If you got this sentence completion on your SAT and tried to solve it using the "sounds good" method, you might get to the answer eventually, but, as you can see, Thelma made sure that nearly all the answer choices sound good. Instead of wasting your time (and walking into Thelma's traps on hard sentences), you need to take the sentence apart much the way Thelma put it together: Find the "clue" she inserted when she wrote the question, and you'll be able to quickly find her answer.

Let's help Thelma finish writing another sentence completion. Here's the sentence she wrote:

2. Historical buildings in many American cities, rather than being destroyed, are now being _____.

(A)
(B)
(C)
(D)
(E)

Do you see which part of the sentence is a clue from Thelma? She's talking about historical buildings, and she's saying that "rather than being destroyed," the buildings are now being—what? Think of the answer in your words. "Fixed" or "restored" would be good answers. Thelma thought of those, and then she looked in her thesaurus to find a harder word. What's a good vocabulary word that means "fixed" or "restored"? Renovated. This is her correct answer.

2. Historical buildings in many American cities, rather than being destroyed, are now being _____.

(A)
(B)
(C)
(D) renovated
(E)

Now let's help her fill in wrong answer choices. We need answers that have to do with buildings being either built or destroyed (since not all testers will pick up on the "rather than" part of the sentence). How about words like "constructed," "designed," or "condemned"? They all fit nicely with the sentence:

2. Historical buildings in many American cities, rather than being destroyed, are now being _____.

(A) condemned
(B) constructed
(C)
(D) renovated
(E) designed

Now Thelma only has to fill in one more word and she's finished another sentence completion (glad we could help, Thelma). What's the point of this exercise? By examining how a sentence completion is made, you learn how to solve it efficiently and accurately. Find the test writer's clue, and you'll know what word she wants.

DO YOU HAVE A CLUE?

All SAT sentence completions contain definite clues as to what word the test writer wants in the blank. They have to—otherwise students could make a case for more than one right answer. For example, look at the following sentence:

The woman told the child, "You're very ____."

(A) friendly
(B) smart
(C) unruly
(D) late
(D) sick

What's the answer? It could be any of the choices. You can't tell which choice is best because there is no clue in the question. This would never be a sentence completion on the SAT. But what if we changed one word:

The doctor told the child, "You're very ____."

(A) friendly
(B) smart
(C) unruly
(D) late
(E) sick

Now what's the answer? It must be sick, because that's the only word of the five that a doctor would say to a child. The word doctor is the clue that tells you what must go in the blank. What happens if we change the clue?

The intelligence tester told the child, "You're very ____."

(A) friendly
(B) smart
(C) unruly
(D) late
(E) sick

What would an intelligence tester say to a child? You're very smart—that's what intelligence testers talk about. By inserting a different clue, you change the meaning of the sentence and therefore change the correct answer.

FIND THE CLUE

By finding the clue in each sentence, you can tell exactly what word Thelma (or whoever wrote your test) wants in the blank. Try underlining the clue in the following sentence completion:

> Although the critics agreed that the book was brilliant, so few copies were sold that the work brought the author little _____ reward.

What's the clue in this sentence? "So few copies were sold." If few copies were sold, what does that mean for the author? She didn't make much money. Or, to phrase it the way the sentence does, the book "brought the author little money reward."

Now, you're probably thinking, "That doesn't sound like good grammar." And you're right. Your word may not sound perfect, but it's perfect enough to get you to Thelma's answer. Look at her answer choices and find the one that is closest to "money":

(A) academic
(B) theoretical
(C) financial
(D) informative
(E) professional

The closest one is obviously C. Easy, huh? Knowing "the answer" before you look at the answer choices helps you find the answer quickly and easily.

ANSWER BEFORE YOU ANSWER

When doing sentence completions, the key is to answer the question in your own words before you look at the answer choices. On every Sentence Completion you do, cover the answer choices before you read the sentence so that you are not tempted to look at them before you come up with your own word. Try the following example. Read the sentence, underline the clue, and then fill in your own word:

> Some developing nations have become remarkably _____, using aid from other countries to build successful industries.

Having trouble finding the clue? Try this: Ask yourself first, "What does the blank refer to?" Then ask, "What else does the sentence say about that same thing?" In the above example, what does the blank refer to? Developing nations. What else does the sentence say about developing nations? They have been able to build successful industries. This phrase is the clue in the sentence because it refers to the same thing the blank refers to.

So, knowing that the countries were able to build successful industries, what word could you put in the blank? The nations have become remarkably what? Successful is a good choice. You don't need to think of another word that means successful—the clue itself gave you a great word, so just fill it in. Take your pencil and write the word "successful" above the blank. Then evaluate each answer choice:

> Some developing nations have become remarkably______, using aid from other countries to build successful industries.
>
> (A) populous
> (B) dry
> (C) warlike
> (D) prosperous
> (E) isolated

(A) Does *populous* mean *successful?* No. Cross it off. Remember POE? Cross off all answer choices that are not close to your word, then deal with any that remain.

(B) Does *dry* mean *successful?* Not at all. Cross it off.

(C) Does *warlike* mean *successful?* Cross it out.

(D) Does *prosperous* mean *successful?* It sure does. Keep it.

(E) Does *isolated* mean *successful?* No. Cross it off.

The answer must be (D).

I Wanted to Find a Clue, But...

Some sentences not only give you a clue, but also give you what we call a trigger word that tells you the direction of the sentence. Trigger words like *therefore, moreover,* and, *and also* indicate that the sentence is staying the same. Trigger words like *but, although, though,* and *however* indicate that the sentence is about to make a change in direction. They tell you, in essence, that the meaning of the sentence is about to change. Look at how a trigger word can affect the direction of a sentence:

Susan is a vegetarian; *moreover,* she refuses to dine with others when they are eating meat.	VS.	Susan is a vegetarian, *but* will eat fish on rare occasions.

The trigger word moreover in the first sentence indicates that the rest of the sentence will say more about how Susan is a strict vegetarian, while the trigger word but in the second sentence indicates that Susan is a vegetarian but in some way she's different. In addition to finding the clue in each sentence completion, you need to be on the lookout for trigger words as well. They too help you to know what word should go in the blank.

Try the following example—underline the clue, circle any trigger words, and write your own word above the blank (I've left out the answer choices so you won't be tempted to read them first):

3. Some anthropologists claim that a few apes have actually learned a rudimentary sign language, but skeptics argue that the apes are only _____ their trainers.

What does the blank refer to? The apes. What else does the sentence say about the apes? That a few have *learned a rudimentary sign language.* This phrase is your clue. Are there any trigger words in this sentence? Yes—just after the clue is the word but, which tells you that the meaning of the sentence is going to change. Therefore, the blank should be somehow opposite in meaning to the clue. So what are the skeptics saying? That the apes haven't really learned sign language; that they are only mimicking or copying their trainers (your answer). Now evaluate each answer choice to see which one is closest to mimicking or copying:

3. Some anthropologists claim that a few apes have actually learned a rudimentary sign language, but skeptics argue that the apes are only _____ their trainers.

(A) imitating
(B) condoning
(C) instructing
(D) acknowledging
(E) belaboring

(A) Does *imitating* mean *mimicking* or *copying?* It sure does. Check the others quickly.

(B) Does *condoning* mean *mimicking* or *copying?* No. Cross it off.

(C) Does *instructing* mean *mimicking* or *copying?* No. Cross it off.

(D) Does *acknowledging* mean *mimicking* or *copying?* No—get rid of it.

(E) Does *belaboring* mean *mimicking* or *copying?* Nope.

The answer is (A).

Why Bother?

Did you really need to check all the answer choices if you find your answer right away? Probably. If you are on an easy question and think you've found your answer, quickly scan the other choices. On medium and hard questions, make sure you evaluate each answer choice. Occasionally you may find that there are two words that are a lot like your word, or that somewhere you got a little off track. If you do find more than one possibility, go back to the sentence, make your word more specific, and then check those choices again to see which is best.

WHERE DID THAT OTHER BLANK COME FROM?

Let's look at another example:

> 5. Sadly, many tropical rain forests are so _____ by agricultural and industrial overdevelopment that they may _____ by the end of the century.

Notice something different? A little more than half the sentence completions on the SAT have not one blank but two blanks. Don't sweat it—just solve the question one blank at a time. Which blank should you do first? Whichever one is easier for you.

Let's take apart the above example. The first word is sadly, which tells you right away what the tone of the sentence is going to be. These little hints can be a big help. What do the blanks refer to? Tropical rain forests. What else does the sentence say about tropical rain forests? This a little tricky, because if we knew the word in the second blank, it would tell us more about the rain forests. If you can't find a good clue, then ask yourself, "What's the story here? What is going on in this sentence?" In this example, industrial overdevelopment is going on. If there is, sadly, a lot of industrial overdevelopment, what may happen to the rain forests by the end of the century? They may disappear—here's your word for the second blank. Now, without filling in the first blank, check all the second words in the answer choices to see which are close to the word disappear:

(A) ???? . . separate
(B) ???? . . vanish
(C) ???? . . expand
(D) ???? . . diminish
(E) ???? . . disappear

(A) Does *separate* mean *disappear*? Not really. Cross off the entire answer choice. It doesn't matter what the first word is if the second word is wrong.

(B) Does *vanish* mean *disappear*? Yes, so keep it as a choice.

ross off this answer choice.

ıld. This may be not be as good a choice as
the first word.

iously, yes. Keep it.

d you're only halfway through doing the ques-
: with a word. Ask yourself the following ques-
agricultural and industrial overdevelopment?"
me, or generally "made bad." If you can't come
: a concept will also work. Using our group of
wer choices that you have not crossed off:

(D) augmented . . diminish
(E) rejuvenated . . disappear

(B) Does *threatened* mean something like *damaged, overcome* or *made bad?* Yes. Keep it and check the others.

(D) Does *augmented* mean *damaged, overcome,* or *made bad?* If you don't know, stash this word and leave the answer choice.

(E) Does *rejuvenated* mean *damaged, overcome,* or *made bad?* No.

You've narrowed it down to two answer choices. What now? Guess. You've done a lot of work and can take a smart guess between two good possibilities. Just to help you get started on your Vocab Stash, augmented means to make bigger, so it does not mean damaged, overcome, or made bad. The answer is (B).

One at a Time, Please

Even if you come up with both words on a two-blank sentence completion right away, you should still check one word at a time. It is much easier to scan a list of words and think, "Does that mean this?" than to read and process each pair of words together: "Does this mean this and does that mean that?" If you come up with both words immediately, simply choose one and use POE on the answer choices just for that blank. After you've crossed off all the answer choices you can, check the remaining choices for the other blank.

GIVE IT A TRY

Put it all together in the following example. Read the sentence and find the clue or clues plus any trigger words. Fill in a word for one of the blanks, then use POE to get rid of answer choices that are not close to yours. Fill in the other blank, then check the remaining answer choices. If you don't know what a word means, you can't cross it off.

6. While the ____ student openly questioned the explanation, she was not so ____ as to suggest that the teacher was wrong.

   (A) complacent . . suspicious
   (B) inquisitive . . imprudent
   (C) curious . . dispassionate
   (D) provocative . . respectful
   (E) ineffectual . . brazen

How did you do? The blanks both refer to the student. In the beginning, the sentence says that the student openly questioned the explanation (that's the clue for the first blank) so a word for the first blank might be questioning or curious. Let's do POE on the answer choices by checking the first words only:

(A) Does *complacent* mean *questioning* or *curious?* Quite the opposite. Cross off answer choice (A).

(B) Does *inquisitive* mean *questioning* or *curious?* It means exactly that, so keep it.

(C) Does *curious* mean *questioning* or *curious?* It sure does. Keep it.

(D) Does *provocative* mean *questioning* or *curious?* Maybe. Keep this choice.

(E) Does *ineffectual* mean *questioning* or *curious?* No. Get rid of it.

You're left with (B), (C), and (D). Now for the second blank. The end of the sentence says that the student was not so something as to suggest that the teacher was wrong. Your clue in this case is the word not, coupled with suggest that the teacher was wrong. What would fit here? Perhaps bold (your word):

(B) Does *imprudent* mean *bold?* If you don't know, you must keep this answer choice.

(C) Does *dispassionate* mean *bold?* No, it means lacking passion. Cross off (C).

(D) Does *respectful* mean *bold?* No, so cross this off.

Even if you don't know what imprudent means, you know (B) must be the answer—it's the only one left, thanks to POE. Don't forget to add imprudent to your stash if you didn't know it.

SENTENCE COMPLETION REVIEW

Are sentence completions now a bit easier then they were a few pages ago? I hope so. Remember the most important rule of sentence completions—fill in the blank(s) with your own word(s) before you check the answer choices—and your accuracy on this question type will soar.

How do you fill in a blank with your own word?

- Find the clue.

  What does the blank refer to?

  What else does the sentence say about the blank?

- Circle any trigger words.

Then what?

- Use POE to get rid of answer choices that are not like your word.
- If you are doing a sentence with two blanks, do one blank at a time.
- Don't forget about Jane Bloggs—she likes words that "sound good"—and remind her of the subject matter in the sentence. How does Jane do on hard questions? She gets them wrong.

ANALOGIES

The key to solving any analogy is to make a sentence with what we call the stem words (the words you're given in the question), and then plug the words from each answer choice into that sentence.

Do you remember from Chapter 4 how Thelma wrote her analogy questions? She chose a pair of stem words that had some sort of definite relationship between them. For the right answer, she chose another pair of words that could fit into the same relationship. Then she filled in the rest of the answer choices. If we approach each analogy the way Thelma wrote them, they will be a snap. Let's try an example:

APPLE : FRUIT ::

Before looking at any answer choices, you need to make a sentence that defines the relationship between the stem words. Your sentence should be simple, clear, and defining. In this case, "*apple* is a type of *fruit*" is a good, clear sentence. "My favorite *fruit* is an *apple*" is not a defining sentence and therefore would not help you get to Thelma's answer. Leave out the subjective stuff and try to make the sentence sound as much like a dictionary definition as possible.

Now that you have a sentence, plug the words from each answer choice into exactly the same sentence to see which pair fits best:

APPLE : FRUIT ::
(A) meal : restaurant
(B) macaroni : cheese
(C) dessert : vegetable
(D) beef : meat
(E) crust : pizza

An *apple* is a type of *fruit*:

(A) Is a *meal* a type of *restaurant*? No. Cross it off.

(B) Is *macaroni* a type of *cheese*? No. Get rid of it.

(C) Is a *dessert* a type of *vegetable*? No. It's outta here.

(D) Is *beef* a type of *meat*? Yes. Keep it.

(E) Is *crust* a type of *pizza*? No.

The answer is (D).

By creating a sentence, and then plugging each answer into that sentence, it's easy to see if the pair of words in the answer choice has the same relationship as the given pair. If you didn't use a systematic approach like this, it would be too easy to get caught up in justifying wrong answer choices. You don't want to find yourself saying, "Well, crust is the outside of the pizza and apples have a crunchy skin on the outside of their fruit... ." Keep it simple and be methodical, and you'll master analogies.

MAKING GOOD SENTENCES

The most important part of doing analogies is making good sentences. Try to begin each sentence with one of the stem words and end the sentence with the other. This will ensure that you aren't putting in a lot of extraneous stuff. Also, try to use words like *is* or *means* to show how one word can be used to define the other.

Remember: Your sentences should be simple, clear, and defining. Try making some sentences for the following examples:

SCISSORS : CUT :: ______________________________

ARCHITECT : BUILDING :: ______________________________

EDUCATION : IGNORANCE :: ______________________________

FAMISHED : HUNGRY :: ______________________________

SHALLOW : DEPTH :: ______________________________

How Did You Do?

Let's look at each of these examples to see how you did:

SCISSORS : CUT ::	Scissors are used to cut *This is a common sentence type on the SAT.*
ARCHITECT : BUILDING ::	Architect designs a building
EDUCATION : IGNORANCE ::	Ignorance means without education *"Means without" is another common SAT-type sentence. It's fine that you switched the order of the words, just remember that you will need to switch the order of the words in each answer choice when you check them.*
FAMISHED : HUNGRY ::	Famished means extremely hungry *This is another common sentence type.*
SHALLOW : DEPTH ::	Shallow means without depth *Yet another common sentence type.*

What Comes Next?

Once you've made a good sentence, what do you do? Plug each answer choice into your sentence and cross off the choices that don't make sense. For example:

SCISSORS : CUT :: scissors are used to cut

(A) lawn mower : slice
(B) glass : pour
(C) glue : cover
(D) joke : amuse
(E) beverage : cleanse

(A) Is a *lawn mower* used to *slice*? Not really, so cross it off.

(B) Is a *glass* used to *pour*? While a glass is occasionally used to pour, this sentence is clearly not the definition of a glass. Don't tie yourself into knots trying to make the choice fit the sentence, like saying "you can *pour* something into a *glass*." If the choice doesn't fit in your sentence, cross it off.

(C) Is *glue* used to *cover*? No, it's used to stick things together. Get rid of it.

(D) Is a *joke* used to *amuse*? Yes, that is the purpose of a joke. Never mind that some jokes just aren't funny. If you looked up *joke* in the dictionary, the definition would probably include the word *amuse*. Keep it.

(E) Is a *beverage* used to *cleanse*? No. Cross it off.

The answer must be (D).

NOW YOU'RE GETTING IT

Are you starting to get a feel for analogies? They can be a little tricky, so let's try a few slightly harder examples, where you don't even know some of the words in the answer choices. Write a sentence for the following pair of stem words:

DEHYDRATE : WATER :: ________________________________

What sentence did you write? How about "Dehydrate means to lose water." You might never say it that way in real life, but the sentence is simple and accurate. Now let's plug in the answer choices.

DEHYDRATE : WATER :: dehydrate means to lose water

(A) polish : gloss
(B) soak : liquid
(C) ???? : steel
(D) rise : ????
(E) ???? : color

(A) Does *polish* mean to lose *gloss?* No, just the opposite. Cross it off.

(B) Does *soak* mean to lose *liquid?* Opposite. Get rid of it.

(C) Oh, no—the first word is a word you don't know. Can we still check this answer choice? Sure, if you know the other word. Can *anything* mean to lose *steel?* Even though I don't know the first word, I don't think there is any word that means to lose steel. Cross this answer off.

(D) Here we go again, another word you don't know. Could *rise* mean to lose *something?* Rise doesn't have anything to do with losing; it might have to do with gaining, but not losing. Cross it off.

(E) One more time (better start studying that vocabulary!): Could *something* mean to lose *color?* Sure, a word that means something like *fade.* This is our best guess at the answer, and in this case it's right.

You got the right answer on this last question without even knowing all the words, thanks to your good defining sentence and POE. Think about how amazing that is—this test is so standardized that you can get right answers using only partial information, as long as you understand how the test is written. Is it easier when you know all the words? Of course. But can you get to the right answer without knowing all the words? Absolutely—you just did.

I Don't Have the Words

Try another example:

????: WIND DIRECTION ::

I know what you're thinking—"How can I make a sentence if I don't know the words?" True, true. But don't forget that you know how Thelma wrote the question.

You can't make a sentence of the stem words, but you know that the words are related in a clear, defining way. Therefore, you know that the right answer has that same clear, defining relationship. You also know that, while Thelma put in a few good runner-up answer choices, she also threw in some really ugly answer choices because she needed to get on with writing more questions. If you can't make a sentence with the stem words, go straight to the answer choices and decide which are the smart guesses and which are not.

Making a Smart Guess

Here's what you do: Read the first answer choice. Can you make a defining sentence with it? If so, make one. If not, cross it off. Try it on the following answer choices:

????: WIND DIRECTION ::

(A) speedometer : pedal
(B) thermometer : water
(C) hourglass : sand
(D) barometer : heat
(E) sundial : time

(A) Can you make a clear, defining sentence with *speedometer* and *pedal*? Not really. If you looked up *speedometer* in the dictionary, you wouldn't see the word *pedal*. Cross it off. If you can't make a sentence with it, it can't be the right answer, no matter what the stem words are.

(B) Can you make a clear, defining sentence with *thermometer* and *water*? Again, not really. Cross it off.

(C) Can you make a clear, defining sentence with *hourglass* and *sand*? Sure. *An hourglass contains sand.* Jot down your sentence and keep this choice.

(D) Can you make a clear, defining sentence with *barometer* and *heat*? No—a barometer does *not* measure heat; it measures pressure. (You've heard the term "barometric pressure," right?) Cross this off.

(E) Can you make a clear, defining sentence with *sundial* and *time*? Sure. *A sundial shows time.*

Without knowing one of the given words, you have just narrowed your answer choices down to two. That's a fifty-fifty shot. Either answer choice would be a smart guess.

Since you do know one of the stem words, let's check each remaining choice against what we know.

???? : WIND DIRECTION ::

~~(A) speedometer : pedal~~
~~(B) thermometer : water~~
(C) hourglass : sand   is in an
~~(E) barometer : heat~~
(F) sundial : time   a sundial shows time

(C) Could something contain wind direction? I don't think so.

(E) Could something show wind direction? Sure, something like a weather vane. (E) is your best guess, and it's the right answer.

WHAT AM I LOOKING FOR AGAIN?

Let's review. If you know the stem words in an analogy, make a clear, defining sentence, and then plug in the answer choices and cross off those that don't fit. If you don't know one or both of the stem words, go directly to the answers and cross off any answer choices that don't have a clear, defining relationship—in other words, any pair of words for which you cannot make a good sentence. Let's try another one:

???? : ???? ::

(A) lava : volcano
(B) center : circle
(C) archipelago : islands
(D) zealot : observer
(E) maverick : herd

Since you cannot make a sentence, what can you do? Go to the answer choices and cross off those for which you cannot make a clear, defining sentence.

(A) Can you make a clear, defining sentence with *lava* and *volcano*? Sure—*lava comes out of a volcano*. Keep this choice.

(B) Can you make a clear, defining sentence with *center* and *circle*? Not really. Circles have a center, but so what? It's not really part of their definition. Cross it off.

(C) Can you make a clear, defining sentence with *archipelago* and *islands*? If you know both words. *An archipelago is a group of islands*. If you don't know the word *archipelago*, you have to keep the answer choice anyway.

(D) Can you make a clear, defining sentence with *zealot* and *observer*? Not really. A zealot is someone who is over-the-top enthusiastic about something, and an observer is someone who watches. Unrelated. If you didn't know the word *zealot*, you would have to keep this choice.

(E) Can you make a clear, defining sentence with *maverick* and *herd*? Again, not really (if you know the word). A *maverick* is a non-conformist, someone who goes against the crowd, but unless you want to refer to the crowd as a *herd* (which is a stretch) these words are unrelated. Cross this choice off.

You know the answer is either (A) or (C) even though you have no idea what the given words are. Pretty wild, huh? Using what you know about Analogies and POE, you can take a smart guess and stand a good chance of getting this question right.

SPEAKING OF HARD ANALOGIES

How do you think our friend Jane is faring with analogies? You know those last few were really tough for her. She doesn't know anything about making a sentence or deciding whether a pair of words would make a good potential answer choice. She does every analogy the same way: "THIS is to THAT: this is to that, this is to that, this is to that, this is to that, this is to that. Hmmm..." Jane gets slammed on vocabulary on the hardest analogies and falls for all the traps by trying to pick an answer choice that reminds her of the stem words. What do you think is Jane's choice in the following example?

INFINITESIMAL : SIZE ::

(A) trifling : significance
(B) distant : galaxy
(C) cacophonous : music
(D) lucid : behavior
(E) enormous : mountain

She's all over (E) because the only word she knows out of the stem words is SIZE. If you were doing this analogy, would you pick (E)? No way, because the words here are too easy, and because hard questions have hard answers. What other answer choices can you get rid of? (B). Distant and galaxy are simple words that don't have a defining relationship, so cross `em off. If you have no idea what INFINITESIMAL means, and don't know at least one word in each of the remaining choices, you can still take a smart guess. What's the right answer? (A). Infinitesimal means small in size and trifling means small in significance (if you don't know these words, be sure to stash 'em). Did you guess right? If you didn't, no big deal—you still guessed smart. The more analogies you do, and the more vocab you learn, the better you'll get at recognizing Thelma's answers.

Analogy Review

To solve analogies, remember the rules:

If you know both stem words

- make a simple, clear, and defining sentence using the stem words
- plug each answer choice into the that sentence
- cross off the choices that don't work

If you only know one stem word

- try to make a clear, defining sentence out of each answer choice
- cross off the answer choices that are unrelated (those for which you cannot make a clear, defining sentence)
- for the remaining answer choices, plug the stem word you do know into the answer choice sentence to see if it's a good guess. Cross off the choices that don't make sense
- make a smart guess
- don't be like Jane!

If you don't know either stem word

- try to make a clear, defining sentence out of each answer choice
- cross off the answer choices that are unrelated (ones for which you cannot make a clear, defining sentence)
- make a smart guess

Critical Reading

The term "critical reading" is a misnomer when it comes to the SAT (add that word to your Vocab Stash if you don't already know it). The definition of read is "to examine or grasp the meaning of the written word." And the term *critical reading* implies that you are not only reading but also making a careful judgment about what you read. SAT critical reading, on the other hand, is primarily about fact-finding. You're not reading to learn something, you're not reading to broaden your perspective, and you're not reading to make an informed evaluation about something. You are reading for only one reason—to answer questions correctly. To answer questions correctly, you need to flip back and forth between the questions and the passage repeatedly, finding the relevant information in the passage and then finding the answer choice that best represents that information. In other words, you need to work the passage, not read it.

The Rules for ETS Writers

When Thelma puts together an SAT critical reading passage, she follows certain rules. She writes or edits a passage so that it contains primarily facts and salient points, with minimal extraneous material (except as deemed necessary to increase the difficulty of a passage). She makes sure that all viewpoints in the passage are reasonably traditional, non-controversial, and politically correct. In other words, her passage is like a bowl of mashed potatoes—bland, innocuous, and acceptable to virtually everyone.

Thelma then creates questions whose answers can be specifically located or clearly derived from the passage. Correct answers are also of the mashed-potato variety—they typically do not contain disputable ideas or extreme language. In addition, there is something clearly wrong with each wrong answer choice, although Thelma tries to be subtle, particularly on more difficult passages.

Now, knowing what you know about how Thelma creates critical reading questions, let's look at one:

29. Lines 39–40 ("Going . . . them") are used to stress

    (A) the laziness of cats that keeps them from being pack animals
    (B) the ignorance of dogs, which makes them more obedient pets
    (C) the antipathy that cats feel for humans
    (D) a difference between cats and dogs that emphasizes the independent nature of cats
    (E) the stubborn and complacent disposition of cats

In this question, Thelma references some lines from the passage. Do you think she's actually telling you exactly where the answer to the question can be found? Not likely.

Here's the line she's referenced:

Going for a walk with a human, therefore, has no appeal for them.

For who? Can you tell what this line is stressing just by reading the line? No. You need to read the sentences before and after the referenced lines to really know what's going on:

So the adult pet dog sees its human family both as pseudoparents and as the dominant members of the pack, hence its renowned reputation for obedience and its celebrated capacity for loyalty. Cats do have a complex social organization, but they never hunt in packs. In the wild, most of their day is spent in solitary stalking. Going for a walk with a human, therefore, has no appeal for them. And as for "coming to heel" and learning to "sit" or "stay," they are simply not interested.

What is the line "Going for a walk with a human, therefore, has no appeal for them" stressing? Cats, unlike dogs, are loners. Using just this information, let's check the answer choices to see which one says something like *cats are loners.*

The sentence is used to stress

(A) *the laziness of cats that keeps them from being pack animals.* Did the passage say that cats are loners because they are lazy? No, so cross it off.

(B) *the ignorance of dogs, which makes them more obedient pets.* This answer doesn't mention cats, so cross it off.

(C) *the antipathy that cats feel for humans.* If you don't know the word "antipathy," you need to keep this choice.

(D) *a difference between cats and dogs that emphasizes the independent nature of cats.* This sounds a lot like "cats, unlike dogs, are loners," and it's a very innocuous (stash that word), mashed-potato type of answer. Keep it.

(E) *the stubborn and complacent disposition of cats.* Even if you don't know what complacent means, you do know that the author's explanation of why cats tend to be loners does not include stubbornness. Cross this off.

You have just narrowed the answer down to two choices, even though you have only read a handful of lines from the passage. Which is your smartest guess? (D), the one that is closest to the answer you came up with. Did you need to read the entire passage to figure out the answer to this question? No. In fact, you practically never need to read an entire critical reading passage. Instead, you need to work the questions and passage smartly in order to get to Critical Reading answers quickly and efficiently.

Critical Working

Step One: Read the Blurb

Prior to each passage, you are typically given a "blurb" about what you are going to read. Some blurbs provide useful clues as to what the passage is about; others are pretty lame. For example:

Useful Blurb	Useless Blurb
In passage 1, the author presents his view of the early years of the silent film industry. In passage 2, the author draws on her experiences as a mime to generalize about her art. (A mime is a performer who, without speaking, entertains through gesture, facial expression, and movement.)	*The following passage is from a book written by a zoologist and published in 1986.*

The first blurb gives you a fair amount of detail about the two passages you will read, while the second tells you practically nothing. Always read the blurb first to see if it tells you anything useful.

Step Two: Work the Questions

Once you've read the blurb, go directly to the questions. Work each question by giving it a quick read and circling or underlining the question part of the question. If the question gives you a line number to refer to when answering the question (and many of them do), flip to the passage, circle the area the question refers to (remember to include about five or so lines above and below the referenced lines), and mark the question number next to that area. If a question does not give you a clue as to where the answer will be located, or is a general question about the passage, circle the question number. Most specific questions are arranged in chronological order, so you're likely to find the answer to a specific question with no line reference by looking in between the lines referenced in the questions just above and just below it. You should answer all general questions about the passage after you answer all the specific questions.

Working the questions should take you no more than a minute or two. You don't need to read the questions in great detail, pondering each one's meaning and studying the potential answers. Instead, you should read just enough of the question to know where to find the answer in the passage. As you do so, you will begin to get an idea of what the passage is about.

Step Three: Answer before You Answer

Remember that the only reason to read a critical reading passage at all is to answer questions. Now that you've worked the questions, only read the parts of the passage for which there is a question.

In most cases, it is helpful to read the first sentence or two of a passage. However, after that, if there are no questions until paragraph three, don't bother reading all of paragraphs one and two. As you read, "step out" of the passage to answer each specific question. In other words, as soon as you read the information that answers one of the questions, go to the question and answer it in your own words.

Try it on the following example. Question 28 refers to the second paragraph of the "cat and dog" passage. As soon as you read the paragraph, answer the question in your own words.

This is rather different from the kind of bond that develops between human and dog. The dog sees its human owners as
Line pseudoparents, as does the cat. On that
(5) score the process of attachment is similar. But the dog has an additional link. Canine society is group-organized; feline society is not. Dogs live in packs with tightly controlled status relationships among the
(10) individuals. There are top dogs, middle dogs, and bottom dogs, and under natural circumstances they move around together, keeping tabs on one another the whole time. So the adult pet dog sees its human family
(15) both as pseudoparents and as the dominant members of the pack, hence its renowned reputation for obedience and its celebrated capacity for loyalty. Cats do have a complex social organization, but they never hunt
(20) in packs. In the wild, most of their day is spent in solitary stalking. Going for a walk with a human, therefore, has no appeal for them. And as for "coming to heel" and learning to "sit" and "stay," they are simply
(25) not interested. Such maneuvers have no meaning for them.

28. It can be inferred from the second paragraph (lines 22–46) that the social structure of dogs is

(A) flexible
(B) abstract
(C) hierarchical
(D) male-dominated
(E) somewhat exclusive

How would you describe the social structure of dogs based on what you read? How about *groups with a pecking order*. Now, read each answer choice to find one that means *groups with a pecking order*:

28. It can be inferred from the second paragraph (lines 22–43) that the social structure of dogs is

    (A) flexible
    (B) abstract
    (C) hierarchical
    (D) male-dominated
    (E) somewhat exclusive

(A) Does *flexible* mean *groups with a pecking order*? No. Cross it off.

(B) Does *abstract* mean *groups with a pecking order*? Nope. Get rid of it.

(C) Does *hierarchical* mean *groups with a pecking order*? Yes. Keep it.

(D) Does *male-dominated* mean *groups with a pecking order*? Careful—there is nothing in paragraph two that talks about gender. Cross it off.

(E) Does *somewhat exclusive* mean *groups with a pecking order*? No. Cross it off.

The answer is (C).

By taking the time to *answer before you answer* (answer the question in your own words before you read the answer choices), checking your answer choices is quick and easy.

Step Four: POE

Step Four is Process of Elimination (POE). Once you've "answered" the question in your own words, you need to go through each answer choice and cross off the answers that are not close to yours. In addition, you can cross off answers that use extreme language (typically a no-no on the SAT) or are just plain stupid based on what you read in the passage. Remember that most of the answer choices you read are wrong. Judge each choice as "wrong until proven right."

Try another question from the "cat and dog" passage. Work the question, read the relevant part of the passage (remember to read above and below the lines referenced), answer before you answer, and then use POE.

The argument will always go on—feline self-sufficiency and individualism versus canine camaraderie and good-fellowship. But it is important to stress that in making a valid point I have caricatured the two positions. In reality there are many people who enjoy equally the company of both cats and dogs. And all of us, or nearly all of us, have both feline and canine elements in our personalities. We have moods when we want to be alone and thoughtful, and other times when we wish to be in the center of a crowded, noisy room.

Line (5) (10)

33. The author uses lines 84–89 ("The argument... positions.") to

(A) show that the argument stated in the passage is ultimately futile.

(B) disclaim glaring contradictions that are stated in the passage.

(C) qualify the generalizations used to make the author's point.

(D) ensure that the reader doesn't underestimate the crux of the passage.

(E) Highlight the differences between individualism and dependency.

In your own words, what is the author using lines 84–88 to do? It sounds like she basically is back-pedaling. She probably made a lot of sweeping generalizations throughout the passage and is now adding in a big disclaimer so that no one can really argue with what she has said. Let's see which of the following answer choices means to *back-pedal*:

The author is using these lines to

(A) *show that the argument stated in the passage is ultimately futile.* This is a little too defeatist and extreme. She is merely qualifying what she's said, not throwing in the towel. Cross this off.

(B) *disclaim glaring contradictions that are stated in the passage.* Again, the language used here is pretty extreme. Remember you are looking for the mashed-potatoes answer.

(C) *qualify the generalizations used to make the author's point.* This is back-pedaling, and it's exactly what she's doing. Plus, it's hard to argue with such a mashed-potato answer. Keep it.

(D) *ensure that the reader doesn't underestimate the crux of the passage.* Does this mean to back-pedal? No. Cross this off.

(E) *Highlight the differences between individualism and dependency.* This answer choice also does not mean to back-pedal. The answer must be (C).

See the Difference?

Do you see how the language used in answer choice (B), "disclaim glaring contradictions," is too extreme to be the right answer, as opposed to the bland language used in answer choice (C), "qualify the generalizations used"? As you eliminate answer choices, be very wary of language that is too strong or extreme, especially if the author's tone in the passage is not at all extreme.

WHERE DO I GO?

As you can see, the line references in most of the specific questions make it easy for you to work efficiently through a passage. But how do you find the answer to a question when there is no line number? By looking in and around the lines that are referenced in the questions just before and just after. Where will you find the answer to question number 27 below?

26. In line 17, the word "pseudoparents" means

27. The author suggests that an important difference between dogs and cats is that, unlike dogs, cats

28. It can be inferred from the second paragraph (lines 22–43) that the social structure of dogs is

Since the answer to question 26 is around line 17, and the answer to question 28 is somewhere within the lines of 22–43, the answer to question 27 will be somewhere in the same vicinity.

WHAT ABOUT THE GENERAL QUESTIONS?

Once you've answered all the specific questions by reading what you need of the passage, answer the general questions. Consider the information you've read, and remember to avoid extreme language. Try this general question from the "cat and dog" passage:

24. The primary purpose of the passage is to

    (A) show the enmity that exists between cats and dogs
    (B) advocate dogs as making better pets than cats
    (C) distinguish the different characteristics of dogs and cats
    (D) show the inferiority of dogs because of their dependent nature
    (E) emphasize the role that human society plays in the personalities of domestic pets

Even though you've only read two of the seven paragraphs of this passage, you still have a basic idea of what it's about: cats versus dogs, cat owners versus dog owners. Using just this information, let's POE:

(A) *show the enmity that exists between cats and dogs.* Since you may not know what *enmity* means, and this answer does talk about cats and dogs, keep it.

(B) *advocate dogs as making better pets than cats.* The author does not explicitly choose one pet over the other. Cross this off.

(C) *distinguish the different characteristics of dogs and cats.* Mashed potatoes. Sounds close. Keep this.

(D) *show the inferiority of dogs because of their dependent nature.* This choice only refers to dogs, and it also puts them down. Cross it off.

(E) *emphasize the role that human society plays in the personalities of domestic pets.* Way too general—the choice should at least *mention* cats and dogs. Cross this off.

You are down to two choices, even though you only read two paragraphs of the entire passage. The answer is (C). Enmity means hatred (stash it), so (A) would be too strong.

SOME ANSWERS ARE JUST BAD

Thelma writes critical reading questions just as she writes other verbal questions: She works hard on the question and correct answer, but less hard on developing wrong answer choices. And, in critical reading, there are a lot of answer choices that are just plain stupid (no offense, Thelma). Look at this question based on the same "cat and dog" passage:

According to the passage, the domestic cat can be described as

(A) a biped because it possesses the characteristics of animals with two feet
(B) a pseudopet because it can't really be tamed and will always retain its wild habits
(C) a contradiction because although it lives comfortably with humans, it refuses to be dominated by them
(D) a soldier because it is militant about preserving its independence
(E) a ruler because although it plays the part of a pet, it actually dominates humans

According to the passage, the domestic cat can be described as

(A) *a biped because it possesses the characteristics of animals with two feet.* Can a domestic cat be described as a *biped*, a creature that walks on two feet? That's pretty ridiculous. Cross this answer choice out.

(B) *a pseudopet because it can't really be tamed and will always retain its wild habits.* Do domestic cats always retain their wild habits? Some may, but it's almost impossible to say that *all* cats *always* do anything. This answer uses extreme wording. Cross it off.

(C) *a contradiction because although it lives comfortably with humans, it refuses to be dominated by them.* This choice is hard to argue with (very mashed-potato), and is also consistent with the answer we chose for question 27. Keep it.

(D) *a soldier because it is militant about preserving its independence.* While not completely ridiculous, this description of a domestic cat as a soldier is a little odd and extreme. Cross this one off.

(E) *a ruler because although it plays the part of a pet, it actually dominates humans.* Although many cat owners joke about being ruled by their cat, this answer is just plain stupid (it's actually rather amusing). Get rid of it.

The only logical answer choice is (C)—and you haven't even checked the passage.

But What About Those Really Hard Questions?

As I mentioned, the questions about a given passage are not set up in a specific order of difficulty, so you are likely to have a mix of easy, medium, and difficult questions. What should you do if you feel like a question is too hard or time-consuming to answer? Skip it, or at least save it for last. We'll talk more in Chapter 7 about exactly how to determine what to skip, but the quick rule of thumb is this: If it's too hard or time-consuming for you, don't do it.

And Then There Were Two Passages

As you know, you will likely have one critical reading passage on your SAT that is actually composed of two passages. These dual passages deal with the same topic but may represent different views or opinions. Typically, you have a bunch of questions about the first passage followed by a bunch of questions about the second passage and finally a few questions about how the two passages relate to each other. Just as you solve two-blank sentence comps one blank at a time, you should also solve dual passages one passage as a time. When you come to a dual passage, read the blurb and then work the questions for the first passage only. Then work passage one and answer the questions before you go on to passage two. Once you finish the passage one questions, work the passage two questions, and then answer them by working passage two. Finally, answer the questions about both passages (remember to answer before you answer and use POE).

You've Got It

Does critical reading seem a bit easier to you? Practicing a few passages will help you master your critical working strategies, so grab your *10 Real SATs* or *Cracking the SAT* and work a few passages. Just remember to work each passage one step at a time:

- **Step One:** Read the Blurb
- **Step Two:** Work the Questions
    - Circle the question part of the question
    - Note in the passage where to find the answer to the question, if possible
    - Circle questions that are general or have no line reference
- **Step Three:** Answer Before You Answer
    - Work the passage, stepping out to answer specific questions as you go
    - Answer the question in your own words before you read the answer choices
    - Answer the general questions and any other tough questions last
- **Step Four:** POE
    - Once you have an answer in mind, use POE to get rid of answer choices that are not close to yours
    - Avoid answer choices that use extreme language
    - Get rid of answer choices that are stupid based on what you've read

Make It Your Own

What if, after practicing, you find it difficult to do some part of critical working? For example, what if you get confused by trying to answer and POE each question as you go, or what if working the questions before you even look at the passage drives you crazy?

If the critical working strategy doesn't completely work for you, modify it until it does. As you know, not everyone learns the same way and not everyone processes information the same way. While the critical working approach is the most efficient and effective way to solve a critical reading passage, you need to make it the best approach for you. Here are two modifications that some girls choose to make to the critical working strategy. If you are having trouble with some aspect of the approach, try one of these modifications.

If you do choose to modify the critical working approach in some way to make it work better for you, just make sure that you are not reverting to a less efficient strategy. Don't choose to read every word of the entire passage and answer each question based on what you remember instead of doing critical working. An approach like that will hold your score down. Instead, try the suggested modifications to see what makes the process a little easier for you.

Modification #1: But I Really Need to Read It

Is reading the questions before you read the passage like trying to ignore an elephant in your bedroom? If the passage's big, gray shadow looms over the questions, demanding your attention and making it impossible for you to concentrate, then do a quick read before you work the questions. Here's how:

Step One: Read the Blurb

Step Two: Read What You Need. Read the beginning of the first paragraph, as far as you feel you must in order to have a clue of what the author is talking about. Once you have a clue about the first paragraph, read the beginning of the second paragraph. This should give you a feel for what the passage is about. Scan the beginning of the remaining paragraphs to see if there is some major change of direction. Do not spend more than 1–2 minutes on this step.

Step Three: Work the Questions

Step Four: Answer Before You Answer

Step Five: POE

Modification #2: I Am So Confused

If stepping out of the passage to answer each question in your own words and then POEing each answer choice makes you lose all sense of what the passage is talking about, try the following modification. This approach will take more time, so only do it if you absolutely need to in order to be accurate:

Step One: Read the Blurb

Step Two: Work the Questions

Step Three: Answer Each Question in Your Own Words. Each time you come to the answer to a question, jot a note of the answer either next to the passage or next to the question. Be sure your note is clear enough to understand when you come back to it. Then go on with the passage instead of doing POE on that question. Answer all the specific questions this way.

Step Four: POE All Questions. Once you've answered all the specific questions in your own words, go back and POE each question. Then do the general questions by answering before you answer and using POE.

When making modifications to your SAT critical working approach, remember these important points:

- SAT critical reading is about answering questions, not about reading the passage.
- Work the passage and questions, going back and forth as much as you need to. All the answers are in the passage; you just need to find them.
- Answer the question in your own words before you read any answer choices—answer choices are designed to confuse, not clarify, so don't rely on them for help.
- Assume all answer choices are "wrong until proven right"—most of them are wrong anyway!
- Write it down—feel free to jot quick notes and circle trigger words or other key words in the passage and questions. Use your writing to keep you focused on your work.

THAT'S IT

You've now learned how to solve each of the three types of questions you'll encounter on the SAT Verbal section. And you've learned the most important rule of solving all SAT verbal questions: get verbal by answering each question in your own words before reading any answer choices. In sentence completions, you get verbal by filling in each blank with your own word, as opposed to trying to figure out which answer choice sounds good. In analogies, you get verbal by putting each pair of stem words into a sentence and then plugging each answer choice into the same sentence. In critical reading, you get verbal by answering before you answer. By taking the time to get a rough idea of the right answer before reading any answer choices, you will avoid many of the traps that Thelma has laid for you throughout the Verbal section of the test.

Your next step is to practice what you have learned. It's easy to practice Verbal right out of 10 Real SATs—do sets of analogies one night, sets of sentence completions the next, and so on. Practice the techniques so that you'll be able to get to the right answers, even when you don't know every word you encounter. And, speaking of words, you better start building that Vocabulary Stash!

Chapter 7
TAKE YOUR TIME

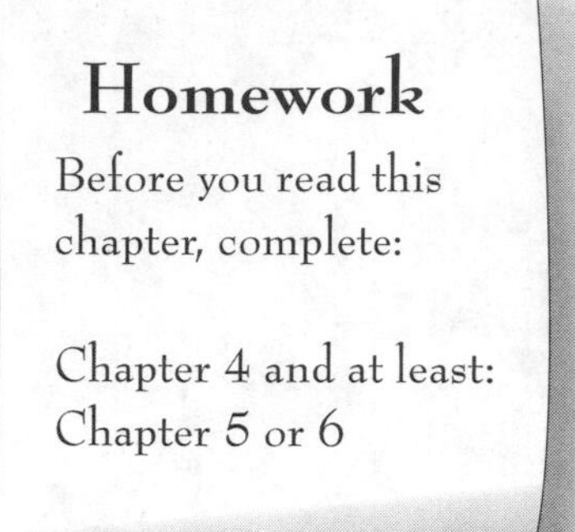

SOLUTION #4: TAKE YOUR TIME

Are the time constraints on the SAT an issue for you? Do you feel as though you could do a whole lot better if you could just take your time? The SAT is a timed test that requires working at an efficient pace, but the fact that it is timed is not worth panicking about. You can learn to take your time on the SAT so that timing is under your control, not vice versa.

This chapter is divided into two parts. In Part I: Find Your Groove, you will find your personal SAT pacing groove by

- determining how many questions you should do on each question type
- learning which questions to skip
- calculating what scores you're currently on target for and how close you are to the scores you really want

In Part II: Improve Your Groove, you will improve your pacing groove by

- learning to maximize your speed in each section without sacrificing accuracy
- maintaining your groove throughout 15-minute and 30-minute sections
- getting the most out of the last five minutes of each section
- sustaining your groove throughout full-length SATs

Don't Do It All at Once

To get the most out of this chapter, don't try to do it all in one sitting. Instead, work through Part I: Find Your Groove over one or two sessions. Once you've finished Part I, take a break from timed work and work on Chapter 8, 9, or 10. When you're ready for more timed work, do the drills in Part II: Improve Your Groove. Also, set aside time to do full-length tests throughout the course of your practice. See the suggested syllabi in the Part II intro to help you plan when to do the drills in the second half of this chapter.

Using *10 Real SATs*

You should be using the tests in *10 Real SATs* throughout this chapter. To ensure that you have enough tests to do all the timed work you need, plus a few left over at the end for full-length test-taking, use *10 Real SATs* as follows:

- Use the first two tests in the book for the Find Your Groove drills.
- Set aside the last three tests as full-length timed tests.
- Use two of the remaining five tests to practice each technique untimed, and the other three to do timed drills and timed sections.

You can also purchase the most recently administered exams from ETS for the most up-to-date practice. Finally, if you have *Cracking the SAT,* then you have additional tests to use as practice material and for timed drills.

Part I: Find Your Groove

What to Skip: Advanced Techniques

As you already know, if you're going to skip questions, you should skip the hardest in each section. But how do you know which questions are the hardest? Do you go strictly by the question number, or are there other factors to consider? As you already learned in Chapter 4, the SAT's Order of Difficulty will generally tell you which questions are easy, which are medium, and which are difficult. However, every test taker is different. Your own personal strengths and weaknesses always play a role. You might find a medium question impossible, or a hard question simple. So how do you know what to do and what to skip?

To Do or Not to Do

On each section of the test, do all the easy questions. In addition, plan to do virtually all the medium questions, unless you encounter one that seems extremely hard to you. When it comes to the difficult questions, you should try to do those that are easier *for you.* That may mean doing one hard question, or maybe none, or it may mean doing virtually all of the hard questions, depending on your groove (more on this in a minute). When you get to a hard question, size it up and decide "to do or not to do." If you decide to do the problem, go ahead and solve it. If you decide not to do the problem, skip it and read the next one. Since skipping in Math and Verbal are slightly different, let's take a look at how to determine what to skip for each question type.

What to Skip in Verbal

As you know, verbal questions get harder within each question type—sentence completions go from easy to medium to difficult, then analogies begin again with easy, and so on. The best way to decide what you will skip and what you will do is to consider the strength of your vocabulary. If you have a strong vocabulary, you will want to do as many of the sentence completions and analogies as you can. If you have a weak vocabulary, you will want to skip the harder sentence completions and analogies and spend more time on critical reading questions. Just remember to size up the hardest sentence comps and analogies instead of struggling through something that's too tough. There are easier questions left to do; you don't need to waste your time working on questions that are too hard for you.

What to Skip in Math

On the problem-solving sections, Order of Difficulty flows straight through the section, so you don't have to worry about sizing up the questions until you hit the last third of the section. However, on the quant comp and grid-in Math section, quant comp has its own Order of Difficulty, and grid-ins start over with easy questions. Therefore, the last third of the quant comp questions—numbers 11–15—are hard questions. You should plan to skip the hardest ones because there are easy and medium grid-in questions waiting to be done. Size up those five questions and ask yourself, "to do or not to do." Don't struggle through some tough, tricky quant comp and potentially run out of time when you could have gained more points by doing the easy and medium grid-ins. On grid-ins, do the easy and medium questions, then "do or not do" the hard ones.

How Many Questions Should I Do?

There are actually two answers to the "How many questions should I do?" question. The first answer is: "The number of questions you can currently do (and get right) while working at a focused, directed pace." The second answer is: "The number of questions you need to get right to achieve the score you want." Which of these two numbers represents the number of questions you should do? Both. By that I mean that you need to determine what those two numbers are and then, if they're not the same or nearly the same, work to bring those two numbers together.

Often when an SAT teacher tells a student how many questions to do, she does so by taking the student's past score (or practice score), tacking on a certain number of points, and then figuring out how many questions the student needs to answer to get the new score. In many of my classes, I've set the "goal score" for the entire class (since all the students were scoring in the same range) by simply telling the students how many questions to do and how many to skip. My male students have typically taken this information in stride. However, my female students usually had lots of questions: *How do you know that's the right number of questions to skip? What if I do that number of questions and still have more time? What if I end up skipping a question that I might have gotten right?*

This, of course, is what I love about female students. Females always need to know the why behind everything; that's why you're such good critical thinkers, and why you do so well in school. Since this book is for you girls, I'm going to teach you a different way of determining the number of questions you'll do. Besides, setting a goal score based on past SAT scores has never sat well with me—after all, girls' SAT scores are lower than they should be to begin with. Why base your goals on these inaccurate numbers?

To determine the number of questions you should do in each section, and ultimately the scores you'll shoot for, you must first find your SAT pacing groove. Your SAT pacing groove is the fastest pace at which you can currently work while still getting most of the questions you do right. The first part of the Take Your Time solution is to determine how much time you need to be accurate in each section. Determining the number of questions you can do while working in your groove will tell you the scores you are currently on target for. You can then see how close those target scores are to the scores you want. Part II of this chapter is about improving your groove—gradually increasing your speed without sacrificing your accuracy—so that the scores your groove puts you on track for become the same as your goal scores.

FINDING YOUR SAT PACING GROOVE

To find your SAT groove, you need to figure out how much time you need to work accurately and efficiently through each set of questions in each section of the SAT. To do so, you must first remove the time constraint altogether. Why? Because you need to find your natural pacing groove before you can start trying to keep pace with the test.

To find your natural pacing groove, work through a few sets of each question type for each section of the test. On each set of questions, note your start time, then work in a focused, directed manner through the set. When you finish the set, note the time, then check your accuracy—how many question you got right, how many you got wrong, how many questions you skipped, and how many of your errors were careless mistakes. Next, adjust your pacing: If you finished quickly but made a lot of careless errors, slow down; if you got everything right but it took you half an hour, speed up. Then do the next set.

What Do You Mean by Accurate?

Working at your most efficient, accurate pace does not necessarily mean the pace at which you never get a question wrong. On a test like the SAT, you'll probably always get a few questions wrong, even if you work slowly and carefully. Instead of striving for no errors, strive for no careless errors. When you check you work after doing a set of questions, examine each question you got wrong to see if you really didn't know the answer or if you just made a careless mistake. Your most efficient, accurate pace will be the fastest pace at which you can work without making any *careless* errors.

The Finding My Groove charts will help you determine exactly how long you need to work accurately through each set of questions within a section. These charts will take you question type by question type, section by section, through the entire SAT—two SATs, actually. Use the first two tests from 10 Real SATs to find your pacing groove.

Finding Your Verbal Pacing Groove

Finding Your Groove in Sentence Completions

To find your sentence completion groove, first do two sets of nine sentence completions (from a 30-question Verbal section in *10 Real SATs*). For each set, note your start time, then work through the set in a focused, directed manner, skipping any problems you would skip on the real test. When you finish the set, note the time, and check to see how accurate you were. Adjust your pace accordingly, and then do the next set. By the time you complete the second set, you will begin to feel your groove—the most efficient pace at which you can work through sentence completion questions while being as accurate as you can. Once you start to feel your groove for nine sentence completions, get a handle on your groove for ten sentence completions (in a 35-question verbal section) by doing two sets of ten sentence completions in the same manner. Use the bottom row of the chart to summarize your groove by indicating about how long it takes you to do sets of nine sentence completions and sets of ten sentence completions, plus how many you typically get right, get wrong, and skip.

My Sentence Completion Groove (allow yourself about 45 minutes of uninterrupted time to do this)							
Question Type	Start Time	End Time	How Long?	Right	Wrong	Skipped	Careless Errors
30-Question Section (30 minutes)							
9 Sentence Completions							
9 Sentence Completions							
35-Question Section (30 minutes)							
10 Sentence Completions							
10 Sentence Completions							

9 Sentence Completions take about how long?	Typical Results?			10 Sentence Completions take about how long?	Typical Results?		
	right	wrong	skip		right	wrong	skip

FINDING YOUR GROOVE IN ANALOGIES

To find your analogies groove, do a few sets of six analogies (30-question section) and then a few sets of thirteen analogies (35-question section) the same way you did the sentence completions—note your start time, work in a focused and directed manner through each set (skipping what you would on a real test), note your end time, check your accuracy, and adjust your pacing. Use the bottom row of the chart to summarize your groove by indicating about how long it takes you to do sets of six analogies and sets of thirteen analogies, plus how many you typically get right, get wrong, and skip.

My Analogies Groove (allow yourself about 45 minutes of uninterrupted time to do this)							
Question Type	Start Time	End Time	How Long?	Right	Wrong	Skipped	Careless Errors
30-Question Section							
6 Analogies							
6 Analogies							
35-Question Section							
13 Analogies							
13 Analogies							

6 Analogies take about how long?	Typical Results?			13 Analogies take about how long?	Typical Results?		
	right	wrong	skip		right	wrong	skip

FINDING YOUR GROOVE IN CRITICAL READING

To find your critical reading groove, do two sets of critical reading from the 30-question Verbal section, then do two sets of critical reading from the 35-question Verbal section. As before, note your start time, and work in a focused, directed manner, skipping what you would on a real test. When you finish, note your end time, check your accuracy, and adjust your pacing. You should also find your groove on the 15-minute Verbal section. The difference, of course, is you know you have 15 minutes to do each section. Don't rush just because the clock is ticking—your goal is to see how many questions you can do in the amount of time you're given without sacrificing accuracy.

My Critical Reading Groove (this drill takes about 90 minutes—can be done in 30-minute segments)							
Question Type	Start time	End Time	How Long?	Right	Wrong	Skipped	Careless Errors
30-Question Section (30 minutes)							
Critical Reading							
Critical Reading							
35-Question Section (30 minutes)							
Critical Reading							
Critical Reading							
15-Minute Section							
Critical Reading	15 minutes						
Critical Reading	15 minutes						

Typical Results								
30-Question Section			35-Question Section			15-Minute Section		
How Long?			How Long?					
right	wrong	skip	right	wrong	skip	right	wrong	skip

Verbal Strategy and Checkpoints

Since you only have 30 minutes for the two longer Verbal sections, you need to decide, based on your work, where your time is best spent. For example, if you were most accurate on sentence comps and analogies, shave the excess minutes off critical reading by planning to skip more of those questions. If, on the other hand, critical reading is your strength, plan to skip one or two more sentence completions and analogies so that you have enough time for critical reading without exceeding 30 minutes. To make these adjustments, do an entire (timed) 30-minute verbal section. Note your start time, and also note the time at which you moved on to each new question type. Once you finish the section, check your accuracy. If necessary, adjust your pacing and then do another thirty-minute section timed. Your goal is to determine your optimal pacing strategy for verbal.

Once you feel you know your optimal verbal pace, fill in the chart below with the number of questions you plan to do for each question type, plus the number of minutes you think you'll need for each type. The time you need for each question type will serve as a checkpoint for you as you do timed work. For example, if you know that it typically takes you nine minutes to do eight sentence completions, and you began a section at 10:00 A.M. and finished the sentence comps by 10:09 A.M., you know you are working right on time. If, instead, you began at 10:00 A.M. and finished the sentence completions at 10:12 A.M., you know you are pacing too slowly.

MY VERBAL STRATEGY

Section	I will do____questions; my checkpoint is____minutes					
	Sentence Comps		Analogies		Critical Reading	
30 Minutes 9 Sent Comps 6 Analogies 15 Critical Read	# of questions	Minutes	# of questions	Minutes	# of questions	Minutes
30 Minutes 10 Sent Comps 13 Analogies 12 Critical Read						
15 Minutes 13 Critical Read						15 min

VERBAL TARGET SCORE

After you determine your groove in each Verbal section, total up the number of questions you're typically getting right, the number you're typically getting wrong, and the number you're skipping in each section. Use these numbers to calculate your potential raw score, and then use an SAT Score Conversion Table (see the end of this chapter) to see what Verbal score you're currently on target to reach.

Typical Performance on Verbal					
Right:		Wrong:		Skip:	
Typical number of questions right	–	$\frac{1}{4}$ × typical number wrong	=	Raw score	Initial target score in Verbal (see Score Conversion Table)
	–		=		

What's Your Verbal Goal Score?

Is the score you're on track for in Verbal the score you want, or were you hoping for something better? If you have a specific goal score in mind, use the following goal score chart to determine what your raw score needs to be to achieve that goal. Your raw score represents the number of questions you need to get right without mistakes. By now you have a feel for about how many mistakes you tend to make, so add about five to ten questions to the raw score to allow for errors. Then get to work on improving your groove by doing the drills and exercises in Part II of this chapter.

VERBAL GOAL SCORE

Score I really want in Verbal	Raw score I need to get it (from Score Conversion Table)	Additional questions to offset mistakes (5 questions allows for 4 mistakes)	=	Number of questions I need to do to get my goal score
		+	=	

Am I Being Reasonable?

How do you know if the score you want is a reasonable goal to shoot for? While anything is possible with a lot of hard work, a goal score that is hundreds of points higher than your target score may be a little unreasonable. The best way to work toward achieving your personal best score is to slowly increase the speed with which you can accurately solve problems. If your goal score is significantly higher than the score you're currently on target for, choose a goal that is somewhere in between the two. If and when you reach that goal score, you can increase your goal and keep practicing.

Finding Your Math Pacing Groove

To find your pacing groove on the 30-minute problem solving section, first do two sets of easy questions (from a 30-minute problem solving section in *10 Real SATs*). For each set, note your start time, then work through the set in a focused, directed manner. When you finish the set, note the time, and check to see how accurate you were. Adjust your pace accordingly, and then do the next set. By the time you complete the second set, you will begin to feel your groove—the most efficient pace at which you can work through easy math questions while being as accurate as you can. Once you start to feel your groove for the easy math questions, get a handle on your groove for the medium-level math questions by doing two sets of medium questions in the same manner. If you come across a medium-level math question that is too hard for you, put a circle around it and skip it. Once you determine how much time you need to do the easy and medium questions, you'll know how much time you have left for the hard questions. Work the hard questions in that amount of time, deciding "to do or not to do" for each question. See how many you do accurately in the time you allotted. Afterward, adjust your pacing—slow down if you did all the hard questions and got most of them wrong; speed up if you did only two hard questions and got both of them right. Then do another set of hard questions. Repeat the same process for the 15-minute problem solving section. Use the bottom row of the chart to indicate your typical performance on each section of the test.

My Problem Solving Groove (this drill takes about 90 minutes—can be done in shorter segments)							
Question Type	Start Time	End Time	How Long?	Right	Wrong	Skipped	Careless Errors
30-Minute Section							
1–7 Easy Questions							
1–7 Easy Questions							
8–17 Medium Questions							
8–17 Medium Questions							
How much time do you have to do the hard Math questions? (30 minutes minus the time it took to do the easy and medium questions)							
18–25 Hard Questions	_____minutes						
18–25 Hard Questions	_____minutes						
15-Minute Problem Solving Section							
1–3 Easy Questions							
1–3 Easy Questions							
4–7 Medium Questions							
4–7 Medium Questions							
How much time do you have to do the hard Math questions? (15 minutes minus the time it took to do the easy and medium questions)							
8–10 Hard Questions	_____minutes						
8–10 hard Questions	_____minutes						

30-Minute Section Results			15-Minute Section Results		
right	wrong	skip	right	wrong	skip

Finding Your Groove on the Quant Comp/Grid-in Section

To find your quant comp/grid-in groove, do two sets of quant comps the same way as you did the problem solving sets—note your start time, work in a focused and directed manner through each set, note your end time, check your accuracy, and adjust your pacing. Remember to skip any medium quant comps that are hard for you, and to evaluate the hard quant comps (numbers 11–15) to decide "to do or not to do." Repeat the process for grid-ins (don't forget "to do or not to do"). Use the bottom row to indicate your typical results.

<table>
<tr><th colspan="8">My Quant Comp/Grid-In Groove
(allow yourself about 60 minutes of uninterrupted time to do this)</th></tr>
<tr><th>Question Type</th><th>Start Time</th><th>End Time</th><th>How Long?</th><th>Right</th><th>Wrong</th><th>Skipped</th><th>Careless Errors</th></tr>
<tr><td colspan="8">30-Minute Section</td></tr>
<tr><td>Quant Comp</td><td></td><td></td><td></td><td></td><td></td><td></td><td></td></tr>
<tr><td>Quant Comp</td><td></td><td></td><td></td><td></td><td></td><td></td><td></td></tr>
<tr><td>Grid-Ins</td><td></td><td></td><td></td><td></td><td></td><td></td><td></td></tr>
<tr><td>Grid-Ins</td><td></td><td></td><td></td><td></td><td></td><td></td><td></td></tr>
</table>

<table>
<tr><th rowspan="2">QC took about how long?</th><th colspan="3">QC Results</th><th rowspan="2">GI took about how long?</th><th colspan="3">Grid-In Results</th></tr>
<tr><th>right</th><th>wrong</th><th>skip</th><th>right</th><th>wrong</th><th>skip</th></tr>
<tr><td></td><td></td><td></td><td></td><td></td><td></td><td></td><td></td></tr>
</table>

Math Strategy and Checkpoints

Though you have pretty much nailed down your groove for the problem solving sections, you still need to clarify what you will do on the Quant Comp/Grid-In section by doing a full-length timed section. This way you can decide, based on your work, where your time is best spent. For example, if you were most accurate on quant comps, shave the excess minutes off grid-ins by planning to skip more of these questions. If, on the other hand, grid-ins are your strength, plan to skip more quant comps so that you have enough time for the grid-ins without exceeding 30 minutes. Do a timed Quant Comp/Grid-In section. Note your start time, then note the time at which you moved from quant comps to grid-ins. Once you finish the section, check your accuracy. If necessary, adjust your pacing, and then do another section timed.

Fill in the chart below with the number of questions you plan to do and the number of minutes you think it will take you to do them. The time you need for each set of questions will serve as a checkpoint for you as you do timed work. For example, if it typically takes you 15 minutes to do quant/comps, and you began a section at 10:00 A.M. and finished quant comps by 10:15 A.M., you know you are working right on time. If instead you began at 10:00 A.M. and finished quant comps at 10:10 A.M., you are probably working too fast.

MY CURRENT MATH STRATEGY

Section	I will do____questions; my checkpoint is____minutes					
	Easy		Medium		Hard	
	#	Minutes	#	Minutes	#	Minutes
30 Minutes 25 Question Problem Solving						
15 Minutes 10 Question Problem Solving						

	Quant Comp				Grid-In			
	Easy	Med	Hard	Minutes	Easy	Med	Hard	Minutes
30 Minutes 15 Quant Comp 10 Grid-In								

TARGET MATH SCORE

Fill in the numbers below, then look up your current raw score on the Score Conversion Table (see the end of this chapter). This is the approximate score you are currently on target to reach.

Typical number of problem solving questions right (30 min. + 15 min. sections)	–	$\frac{1}{4}$ × typical number of problem solving questions wrong	Add this column to get raw score
	–		=
Typical number of quant comps right	–	$\frac{1}{3}$ × typical number of quant comps wrong	
	–		=
		Typical number of grid-in questions right	=
		Raw score	
		Initial target score in math (see Score Conversion Table at the end of the chapter)	

WHAT IS YOUR MATH GOAL SCORE?

If you have a specific Math goal score in mind, use the following chart to determine what your raw score needs to be to achieve that score. Your raw score represents the number of questions you need to get right without mistakes. By now you have a feel for about how many mistakes you tend to make, so add about five to ten questions to the raw score to allow for errors. Then get to work on improving your groove by doing the drills and exercises in Part II of this chapter.

MATH GOAL SCORE

Score I really want in Math	Raw score I need to get it (from Score Conversion Table)	Additional questions to offset mistakes (5 questions allows for 4 mistakes)	=	Number of questions I need to do to get my goal score
		+	=	

As I mentioned in Verbal, if your goal score is much higher than the score you're on track for currently, pick a goal somewhere in the middle and strive to achieve that. You can always raise your goal score, but you don't want your expectations to cause you to push yourself to go too fast too soon. Remember that just doing more questions will not raise your score; getting more questions right will.

WHAT'S NEXT?

You've just completed the first step toward mastering taking your time on the SAT. You should now know

- how many questions you are going to do and how many you are going to skip in each section of the test
- approximately how long it takes you to do each question type within each section (you will use this information as your pacing checkpoints when you do timed work)
- the scores you are currently on target to reach
- how close your target scores are to your goal scores

The next step toward maximizing your efficiency on the SAT is to improve your groove. By doing timed drills, you'll be able to gradually increase the speed with which you can work through a section without sacrificing accuracy. The rest of this chapter is chock-full of drills designed to help you do just that. Throughout the weeks leading up to the SAT, you should do timed work as part of your preparation. The more you work under timed conditions, the better you'll become at slipping into your SAT groove.

Part II: Improve Your Groove

Now that you know what your groove is in both Math and Verbal, it's time to get to work on improving your groove—in other words, honing your skills through timed work so that you can maintain your accuracy while working more efficiently.

The Improve-Your-Groove Drill

This drill is very similar to the one you used for finding your groove. You are going to do several sets of the same question type in a row and gradually try to increase your pace on each set without sacrificing accuracy. Be sure to do the number of questions of each type that you intend to do on the real test (based on the work in did in Part I of this chapter). When you start a set, note your start time. If it typically takes you 11 minutes to do a set of sentence completions, work at a focused, directed pace that is slightly faster to see if you can finish the set in 10 minutes. When you finish, check your work to make sure your accuracy didn't suffer. Make any necessary adjustments, and then do another of the same set.

Do this drill for each of the Verbal question types (remember to skip the number of questions that you plan to skip on the actual SAT). For math, break the sections into quant comps and grid-ins when you have them, and into easy, medium, and difficult on the problem solving sections (again, only do the number of questions you are likely to do on the real test). For all of these sections, work at slowly increasing your speed, but only as long as you maintain your accuracy. Once you successfully increase your speed while maintaining your accuracy, you can try doing some additional questions.

Use the Improve Your Groove Drill chart to keep track of your progress.

Improve Your Pacing Groove

To do the following drill, determine the set of questions you want to do (easy math, easy/medium math, quant comps, sentence completions, analogies, etc.) and how long it typically takes you. Note your start time when you begin the set. Work at a focused, directed pace. Note your end time, then check your accuracy. Make any needed adjustments, and then do another of the same set. Work to increase your speed without getting more questions wrong.

Improve-Your-Groove Drill Chart

Question Set	Start Time	End Time	Minutes it Took	Accuracy			
				Right	Wrong	Skip	Careless Errors

PUT IT ALL TOGETHER

TIMED SECTION DRILL

Now that you've settled into a Math and Verbal groove, you need to do some complete Math and Verbal sections under timed conditions. This time, you need to abide by the start time and end time as if you were taking the real test. Choose a section to do, and set a timer to the allotted time (30 minutes for most sections, 15 minutes for the shorter Math and Verbal sections). Then work through the section as you would on the actual test. When you reach a checkpoint (end of question type), take a quick look at your watch or timer to see if you are pacing yourself properly, and adjust your working speed if necessary.

When you finish the section, check your work to see if you maintained your accuracy. If you did, great! If not, think about why—did you blow through the easy problems too quickly and make some careless mistakes, or were there questions that you just didn't know how to do? Did you begin to lose your focus near the end of the section?

Whatever the cause, see if you can make some adjustments and then try again. I suggest you do a few Verbal sections consecutively, making adjustments and honing your Verbal strategy. Then do the same for Math—do a section, evaluate your work and make the appropriate adjustments, then do a few more sections to lock in your approach. Use the Timed Section chart to keep track of your timed section work.

TIMED SECTION DRILL

Choose a section to do, then set a timer to the allotted time (30 minutes for most sections, 15 minutes for the shorter Math and Verbal sections). Work through the section as you would on an actual test. When you reach a checkpoint, take a quick look at your watch or timer to see if you are pacing yourself properly. Adjust your pace if necessary. When you finish the section, check your work to see if you maintained your accuracy. Make notes on areas you need to work on. Do two to three Verbal sections consecutively. At another sitting, do two to three Math sections. Track your results in the chart below. Do additional timed sections regularly through the rest of your practice time.

TIMED SECTION DRILL CHART

Math/ Verbal	How long? Which section?	How was my pacing?	Accuracy			Notes (what went well, what do I need to work on…)
			R	W	Careless	

FIVE MINUTES LEFT

What's your typical reaction when a proctor announces that there are five minutes left in a section? Many people panic and find it hard to get anything more done. But you can get a lot done on the SAT in only five minutes. You simply need to know exactly how long five minutes is.

Five Minutes Long

Imagine the following scenarios:

- five minutes of those ads for car dealers where the guy screams at you the whole time
- five minutes at a red light on a deserted road at 2 A.M.
- five minutes of a fire siren stuck at its loudest decibel
- five minutes of silence in homeroom
- five minutes on hold with a friend on the other line

I know you're thinking, "Five minutes is five minutes! What's she talking about?" But five minutes is plenty of time to do a few problems on the SAT. The question is how many. Two problems? Three? Four? Two plus a quick look back at an earlier problem? Five minutes shouldn't send you into a panic. It's just another checkpoint for you.

If you're doing a Verbal section, you'll probably be on critical reading when the proctor calls five minutes. In Math, you'll be on either the grid-ins or the medium to difficult problem solving questions. To see how much you can actually do in five minutes on both Math and Verbal, try a few of these five-minute drills. Remember that your accuracy is just as important as the number of questions you do.

5 Minute Drills

Hard Drill. Choose a Problem Solving section, and draw a line separating numbers 17 and 18. If you are only doing 17 or 18 questions, begin at number 12 or 13. Set a timer or have someone time you for five minutes. Beginning at number 18, select the easiest questions for you and do as many as you can in the time allotted. After five minutes, take a one-minute break and then repeat this exercise, choosing from among the problems that you skipped the first time through. Repeat until you've done all the problems that you would choose to do, and then check your work. Did you select the best questions the first time through? The second? Were the ones you chose to skip the first time indeed harder and more time-consuming? Use this information to help you hone your ability to select the best problems for you.

Grid-in Drill. Choose a Quant Comp/Grid-In section, and then draw a line separating questions 20 and 21 if you are only doing up to number 20 or 21 grid-ins begin at number 17). Make sure you have a grid-in answer sheet to practice on. Set a timer or have someone time you for five minutes. Beginning at number 21, select the easiest questions *for you* and do as many as you can in the time allotted. (Use your answer sheet—gridding in answers takes a little longer than just coloring in a bubble.) After five minutes, take a one-minute break and then repeat this exercise, choosing from among the problems that you skipped the first time through. Repeat until you have done all the problems, and then check your work. Did you select the best questions the first time through? The second? Were the ones you chose to skip the first time through indeed harder and more time-consuming? Did you grid-in your answers accurately?

5-Minute Critical Reading Drill: Select a critical reading passage to do and set a timer or ask someone to time you for five minutes. When time begins, read the blurb, then go to the first specific question that has a line reference. Look back to the area around the lines referenced, then use POE to get to the answer. Go to the next specific question with a line reference and repeat the process. Do as many of the line reference questions as you can (focusing on accuracy of course). If you have any extra time, look at the shortest general question, POE what you can based on what you've read, and take a guess.

FULL-LENGTH TESTS

Before every play there's a dress rehearsal; and before every game there's a scrimmage. With good reason—you don't know what it's like to perform in a full-length drama or play a full game until you try it. The same goes for the SAT. You need to practice on a few full-length tests under timed conditions to know what to expect on test day. Do you start off strong but then start to fade? Or does it take you a few sections to get warmed up? Do you need to grab a quick snack on the break so you can concentrate for the full three hours? Taking tests under timed conditions is the only way to be fully prepared on test day.

GET READY

Set aside at least three hours in which you won't be interrupted—preferably in the morning, since you'll take the SAT in the morning. Tear out one of the answer sheets from *10 Real SATs* so you can practice filling in your answers on the answer sheet. Choose a full-length test from *10 Real SATs*, plus an additional section from *10 Real SATs* or *Cracking the SAT* to substitute for the Experimental section (the tests in *10 Real SATs* don't include Experimental sections). Use a timer or ask someone to time you.

GET SET

Before you begin the test, review your current strategy. How many questions should you do in each section? What are your Math and Verbal checkpoints? Make sure you are completely in your SAT groove before you begin.

Go

Do the first three 30-minute sections, and then take a five-minute break. Do the next two 30-minute sections, and then take a two-minute break. Finish with the last two 15-minute sections. Once you're finished, score your test (instructions for scoring are provided in *10 Real SATs* and *Cracking the SAT*).

Once It's Over

How did you do? Are you on or near your goal score? Above it? Below it? How was your pacing? Did you reach your checkpoints on time, or were you working too quickly or too slowly? Were you able to adjust your pacing as you went?

Use the results of this full-length test to adjust your goal scores and zero in on the areas you need to review. Don't just mark an answer right or wrong; go back and see what you did wrong when you made a mistake. As you went through the test, did you make some smart guesses? Did you get those guesses right? Review the material or vocabulary from those questions too so you'll know it if it comes up on your test.

Once you've reviewed your work and adjusted your goals, take another full-length test (not on the same day, of course!). You should plan to take two to three full-length tests before the big day.

SCORE CONVERSION TABLE

Raw Score	Verbal Scaled Score	Math Scaled Score	Raw Score	Verbal Scaled Score	Math Scaled Score
78	800		36	510	560
77	800		35	510	550
76	800		34	500	540
75	800		33	490	530
74	780		32	480	520
73	760		31	480	520
72	750		30	470	510
71	740		29	460	500
70	740		28	460	490
69	730		27	450	480
68	720		26	450	480
67	710		25	440	480
66	700		24	430	470
65	690		23	430	460
64	680		22	420	450
63	670		21	410	440
62	670		20	400	430
61	660		19	390	430
60	660	800	18	380	430
59	650	790	17	380	420
58	640	770	16	370	410
57	640	760	15	360	400
56	630	740	14	350	390
55	620	730	13	350	390
54	620	720	12	340	380
53	610	700	11	330	370
52	600	690	10	310	350
51	600	680	9	300	340
50	600	660	8	290	340
49	590	650	7	270	330
48	590	650	6	270	310
47	580	640	5	230	300
46	570	630	4	230	300
45	570	620	3	230	280
44	560	610	2	230	260
43	560	600	1	230	250
42	550	600	0	230	240
41	550	590	–1	230	220
40	540	580	–2	230	220
39	530	570	–3	230	200
38	530	560	–4	230	200
37	520	560	–5 and below	230	200

Chapter 8
Work Smart, Guess Smart

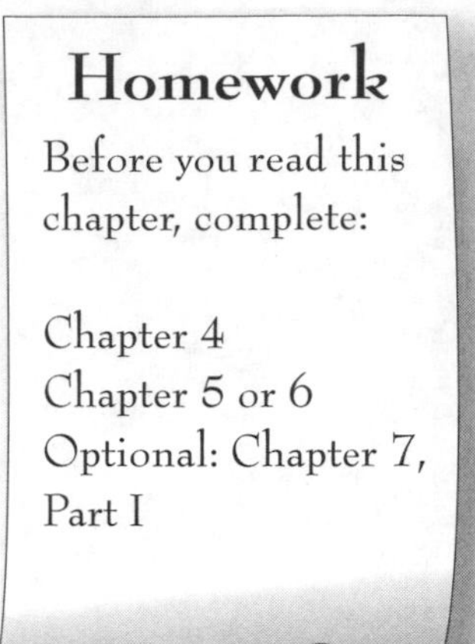

SOLUTION #5: WORK SMART, GUESS SMART

By now you know how different taking the SAT is from doing regular school work—you know that taking shortcuts works to your advantage and that guessing increases your score. You've even seen how you can do very little work and still guess the right answer to both math and verbal questions.

But it's still not easy to do, is it? Many of us remain reluctant to cut corners, even when we know it's the key to higher scores. When we hit a tough question, it's in our nature to hang in there, give it another minute, do some more calculating, and find the right answer the traditional way. We just don't like to give up, take a guess, and move on.

Of course, deep down you know that enlightenment will not come simply from staring at a question a little longer. You also know that by cutting the right corners you'll have more time for the rest of the questions. How can you learn when to take a shortcut, when to keep working at a problem, and when to guess and move on? The same way you've learned to master everything else on this test—by thinking like the test maker rather than the test taker.

In this chapter, we'll look at smart guessing through the eyes of Thelma, the question writer. Your natural tendency to see the big picture will help you as you learn to view questions and answer choices from another level, evaluating them as if you were the test's critic. Specifically, you'll learn to work smart and guess smart by

- putting yourself in the shoes of the test writers so that identifying wrong answers becomes second nature
- practicing working problems the SAT-smart way
- learning to guess smart

You Write the Test

What better way to think like a test writer than to take your turn being one? Let's write some questions together. I'll start with the question, and then we'll create the wrong answer choices. This way you can focus on exactly how Thelma and all those other test writers come up with wrong answers, which will make you more able to spot and eliminate them when you take your test.

5. Six cups of flour are required to make two batches of cookies. How many cups of flour are needed to make enough cookies to fill ten jars, if each jar holds 1.5 batches of cookies?

   (A)
   (B)
   (C) 45
   (D)
   (E)

This is how I wrote it: It takes six cups of flour to make two batches of cookies. How many cups does it take to make one batch of cookies? Three cups. To fill ten jars of 1.5 batches each, you need to make how many batches of cookies? 15. Each batch requires three cups of flour, and 15 (batches) × 3 (cups of flour) = 45.

Now, to fill in wrong answer choices, think about the mistakes that a test taker could make. What if a tester forgot that six cups of flour made *two* batches of cookies? She would assume that you need six cups of flour for each batch of cookies. Another mistake a tester might make is to overlook or forget that one jar holds more than one batch of cookies. She would then assume that only 10 batches of cookies were being made. If a tester makes either of these mistakes, you, the test writer, want to have her wrong answer waiting for her as a trap. On the above problem, fill in some wrong answer choices in light of these two potential mistakes.

Here's what I got:

5. Six cups of flour are required to make two batches of cookies. How many cups of flour are needed to make enough cookies to fill ten jars, if each jar holds 1.5 batches of cookies?

   (A) 90 (6 cups of flour × 15 batches of cookies)
   (B) 60 (6 cups of flour × 10 jars of cookies)
   (C) 45
   (D) 30 (3 cups of flour × 10 jars of cookies)
   (E)

Now you just need to fill in an answer for (E) and we're done. For (E), you want a number that's smaller than 30 (to keep the choices going in descending order). How about 15? 10 jars times 1.5 will give you 15—not that most students will make that mistake, but it works with the rest of our numbers.

As you can see, creating wrong math answers means zeroing in on all the potential mistakes a tester can make. Let's try another:

21. A ball bounces up $\frac{3}{4}$ of the distance it falls when dropped, and on each bounce thereafter, it bounces $\frac{3}{4}$ of the previous height. If it is dropped from a height of 64 feet, how many feet will it have traveled when it hits the ground for the fourth time?

(A) 286
(B)
(C)
(D)
(E)

Here's how I wrote it: The ball first drops 64 feet. Then it bounces up $\frac{3}{4}$ of 64 feet: $\frac{3}{4} \times 64 = 48$. It travels back down 48 feet, hits the ground, then travels up $\frac{3}{4}$ of 48 feet: $\frac{3}{4} \times 48 = 36$. It travels back down 36 feet, hits the ground for the third time, then travels up $\frac{3}{4}$ of 36 feet: $\frac{3}{4} \times 36 = 27$. It travels back down 27 feet and hits the ground for the fourth time. The trip the ball takes looks something like this:

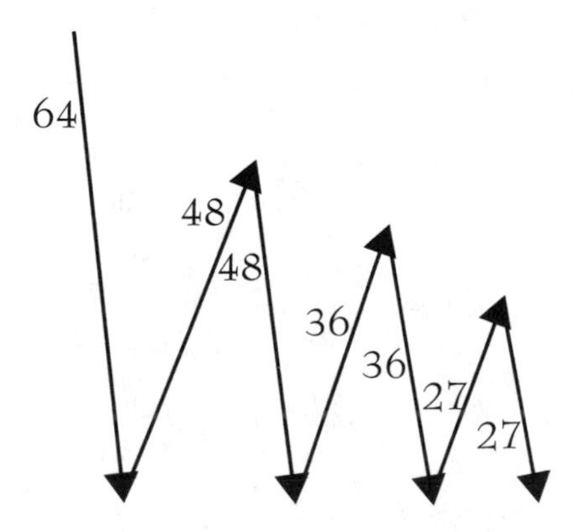

Add up the numbers and you get 286—that's the distance in feet the ball has traveled by the time it hits the ground for the fourth time.

Now for the wrong answers. What mistakes might a test taker make? Some testers will forget to add the distance of both the up trips and the down trips. Some testers will add only four legs of the ball's journey as opposed to when the ball hits the ground for the fourth time. What wrong answers will these mistakes generate? What other mistakes can you think of that would generate tempting wrong answer choices? Fill in what you come up with:

21. A ball bounces up $\frac{3}{4}$ of the distance it falls when dropped, and on each bounce thereafter, it bounces $\frac{3}{4}$ of the previous height. If it is dropped from a height of 64 feet, how many feet will it have traveled when it hits the ground for the fourth time?

(A) 286
(B)
(C)
(D)
(E)

What did you get? The "Jane Bloggs" answer on this hard question is 175—Jane takes $\frac{3}{4}$ of each number, but forgets to add the distances twice (once for up, once for down). 196 is another common wrong answer—this tester adds $64 + 48 + 48 + 36$ and thinks, "I've added up the first four bounces." What other wrong answers did you come up with? 192 is an option for the student who takes $\frac{3}{4}$ of 64 and then multiplies 48×4. 222 is for the student who does all the work correctly but forgets to add in the 64 feet the ball traveled initially.

You get the idea. In Math, answer choices are rarely random—Thelma creates them by figuring out the mistakes students might make. How does this help you when it comes to guessing? By showing you how to spot wrong answer choices. Knowing how Thelma creates wrong answers puts you on the lookout for the mistakes she expects you to make. If you know what Thelma expects you to do, you know what answer choices to avoid.

JUST ASK JANE

Look at this quant comp problem to see what I mean:

	Column A	Column B
13.	The ratio of nickels to dimes in Jar A, where there are 4 more nickels than dimes	The ratio of nickels to dimes in Jar B, where there are 4 more dimes than nickels

What answer is calling your name as soon as you read this problem? "(C), EQUAL!!!" because each column sounds the same if you don't read carefully. Because this is a hard quant comp problem (13 out of 15), can the answer be so obvious? Very unlikely. Now, let's say you really have no idea how to do this problem. If you were Jane, you would either pick (C), or maybe (D), because you're not given numbers for the total of nickels and dimes (How can there be a real answer if there are no real numbers?). So if you, the intelligent test taker, had to guess, what would you choose? (A) or (B). Right there you have a fifty-fifty chance of guessing the right answer. Those are great odds. Remember, you get one point if you're correct and you only lose a fraction of a point if you're wrong. If you can narrow the possible answers down to two choices, you'll improve your score by guessing.

Now Let's Help Thelma with Verbal

SAT answer choices aren't random in the Verbal section either. Since you've already helped Thelma create wrong answers on sentence completions, let's try some critical reading questions.

Here's the first paragraph of a dual critical reading passage, plus the first question and right answer. Let's write in some wrong answer choices that might attract a tester who doesn't know the best way to approach critical reading.

Passage 1

On January 28, 1893, Americans read in their evening newspaper a bulletin from Honolulu, Hawaii. Two weeks earlier, said the news *Line (5)* report, a group of American residents had overthrown a young native queen and formed a provisional government. Marines from the U.S.S. *Boston* had landed at the *(10)* request of the American minister in order to protect lives and property. Violence had ended quickly. The rebels were in full control and were said to have enthusiastic sup- *(15)* port from the populace. Most noteworthy of all, they had announced the intention of asking the United States to annex the islands.

Question

In Passage 1, what event occurred "two weeks earlier" (line 4) than January 28, 1893?

(A)

(B)

(C) American rebels seized governmental control of the Hawaiian Islands.

(D)

(E)

What did you come up with for wrong answers? Choose other things that were discussed in the paragraph or things that are most likely mentioned later in the passage. For example, create an answer choice or two that says that the U.S. annexed Hawaii:

(A) Hawaii became the fiftieth state of the United States.

(B) The United States annexed the Hawaiian Islands.

Thelma also likes to include catchy quotes from a passage, quotes that would easily catch a test taker's eye during a long exam. In the first paragraph, the U.S.S. *Boston* could be used to make a great catchy quote—it stands out from the other text, so it would make a good wrong answer choice. Remember, though, that if you choose to use a catchy quote, you need to make sure your answer is clearly wrong, like this:

(D) Marines from the U.S.S. *Boston* arrived to protect the young native queen from rebels.

That's not why they arrived, so the second half of the answer makes this choice clearly wrong.

Finally, you can make up something that was not said but that some students might infer. For example:

(E) Angry Hawaiian natives rebelled against American rule in Honolulu.

This is a decent wrong answer, because some students would jump to this kind of conclusion. Our critical reading question is now complete:

> In Passage 1, what event occurred "two weeks earlier" (line 4) than January 28, 1893?
>
> (A) Hawaii became the fiftieth sate of the United States.
> (B) The United States annexed the Hawaiian Islands.
> (C) American rebels seized governmental control of the Hawaiian Islands.
> (D) Marines from the U.S.S. *Boston* arrived to protect the young native queen from rebels.
> (E) Angry Hawaiian natives rebelled against American rule in Honolulu.

YOU BE THE CRITIC

Now that you've been the test writer, I want you to go one step further—become the test editor. Imagine that you have test writers turning in potential material to you. How are you going to ensure that the work they've given you is good enough for your test? By confirming the right answer to each question and identifying exactly what makes each wrong answer wrong.

Try being the critic on a critical reading question. This one is about the second passage of the dual Hawaii passages. I've printed the first paragraph of Passage 2 so you can look back for the details. Circle, underline, or jot a note next to each answer choice, explaining exactly why it's wrong (except for the right answer, of course!):

Passage 2

President Cleveland was opposed to annexation throughout his term of office. He believed *Line* taking the islands was immoral, *(5)* and without his support, annexationists had no hope. The Provisional Government, however, did not cease to push its cause in Washington—in fact, *(10)* the vocal commissioner Lorrin Thurston pushed so hard that he was declared persona non grata.

Question 8

Passage 2 suggests that the Provisional Government of Hawaii

(A) often caved in to pressure from the mainland
(B) was merely a puppet of American economic interests
(C) received a large amount of support from the American government
(D) persisted despite resistance from the American government
(E) was completely representative of the people of Hawaii

The answer is (D). The first paragraph says "The Provisional Government, however, did not cease to push its cause in Washington . . . ," even though the president was against annexation. Let's see what made the other answers wrong:

(A) often caved in to pressure from the mainland	opposite of what paragraph says
(B) was merely a puppet of American economic interests	not bad, but too strong a statement
(C) received a large amount of support from the American government	opposite
(D) persisted despite resistance from the American government	true
(E) was completely representative of the people of Hawaii	too strong, not in passage

Now try another critical reading question. Even though you have no passage to refer to, your recent experience as a test writer should tell you which of these answer choices are just not possible. Annotate each answer choice, and then guess which is the most probable right answer:

In Passage 2, the author attempts to

(A) perpetuate out-of-date historical values
(B) justify the reasons underlying a poor decision
(C) correct a misconception
(D) condemn the perpetuators of a deplorable situation
(E) compare two superfluous ideas

You have no idea what the author talked about in Passage 2, but I bet you know what the author did not talk about. Let's go over each choice:

(A) *perpetuate out-of-date historical values.* Would any author perpetuate out-of-date values? That's just kind of stupid, don't you think?

(B) *justify the reasons underlying a poor decision.* This one is worse than (A)—no SAT writer would attempt to justify a poor decision. She might try to explain the underlying reasons for a poor decision. But justify one? Unlikely.

(C) *correct a misconception.* Here's an innocuous answer that's hard to argue with. Keep it.

(D) *condemn the perpetuators of a deplorable situation.* This is a bit extreme for any ETS author. Thelma may criticize, but she generally will not condemn.

(E) *compare two superfluous ideas.* If you know what superfluous means, you know that this is a stupid answer. Something superfluous is extra, unnecessary, almost irrelevant (stash the word if you didn't know it). Why would an author spend time comparing two irrelevant ideas? She wouldn't.

If you were annotating these answer choices, then, they would look like this:

~~(A)~~	perpetuate out-of-date historical values	stupid
~~(B)~~	justify the reasons underlying a poor decision	very stupid
(C)	correct a misconception	sounds possible
~~(D)~~	condemn the perpetuators of a deplorable situation	way too strong
~~(E)~~	compare two superfluous ideas	why bother?

Now let's try annotating a math question. As you solve the following question, try to figure out where each answer choice came from.

23. 250 customers purchased produce from a farm stand in a 4-day period. On the first day, 54 customers purchased produce. On the second day, 39 customers purchased produce. On the third day, c customers purchased produce, and, on the fourth day d, customers purchased produce. If c and d are positive integers, what is the greatest possible value of d?

(A) 54
(B) 93
(C) 156
(D) 157
(E) 250

Before you did any math, you should have crossed off answer choice (E). The question asks for the greatest possible value of d, the number of customers who purchased produce on the fourth day. Can d be as big as 250? No way, because a total of 250 people visited the stand in four days, and you already know that some people came on the first *two* days. d has to be less than 250. Answer choice (E) is for test takers who are either rushing to fill in answers at the end of the test or who are worse test takers than Jane. Cross off (E) as a "worse than Jane" answer choice.

By the way, you can also cross off (A), 54, for a very similar reason. If I had 10 seconds to go, and was skimming hard math questions and taking random guesses, I might pick 54 because it is a number in the problem. We know that Thelma does not want students to be able to randomly guess the right answer, so you know that a number that is in the problem cannot be the answer to a hard question.

Now, as you worked the problem, you probably spotted more "trap" answer choices. To solve the problem, you needed first to figure out how many of the 250 people came on days three and four, and then try a number for c that is as small as possible in order to make d as big as possible. When you add up the number of people who made purchases on days one and two, you get $54 + 39 = 93$. Did you see that trap answer? Next, subtract those people from the 250 total that visited: $250 - 93 = 157$. Did you pick (D)? Jane did. If $d = 157$, that means $c = 0$. But remember the beginning of the last statement: "If c and d are positive integers..." Is 0 a positive integer? No, 0 is neither negative nor positive. So the smallest that c can be is 1. What's the biggest that d can be? $157 - 1 = 156$. The answer is (C).

Your annotated question should look something like this:

23. 250 customers purchased produce from a farm stand in a 4-day period. On the first day, 54 customers purchased produce. On the second day, 39 customers purchased produce. On the third day, c customers purchased produce, and, on the fourth day, d customers purchased produce. If c and d are positive integers, what is the greatest possible value of d?

~~(A)~~	54	in the problem
~~(B)~~	93	total of first 2 days
(C) (circled)	156	that's it!
~~(D)~~	157	Jane's answer—but c cannot be 0
~~(E)~~	250	worse than Jane's answer—don't just pick the biggest number

Do you see how most answer choices are not random, especially on the hardest questions? The more you analyze questions from a critic's point of view, the easier it will be for you to recognize and avoid the tricks and traps set by the test writers.

WORK SMART

Now that you've sat on the test writer's side of the table, solving problems by working smart should be a little easier to do. Let's work smart on some SAT math problems that can virtually always be answered before they are completely solved: quant comp.

Quantitative comparisons are about comparing, not computing. Therefore, to work smart on quant comp, you only need to do enough math to tell which column is bigger, and then use POE to get you to the answer. On the easiest quant comps, you can do this quickly and assertively. Let's review what quant comp answer choices mean, as we discussed in Chapter 5, and then try a few moderately easy quant comps:

A—column A is always, always bigger than column B
B—column B is always, always bigger than column A
C—columns A and B are always, always equal
D—D is for Don't Know

Column A **Column B**

The average of positive integers p and q is 3.

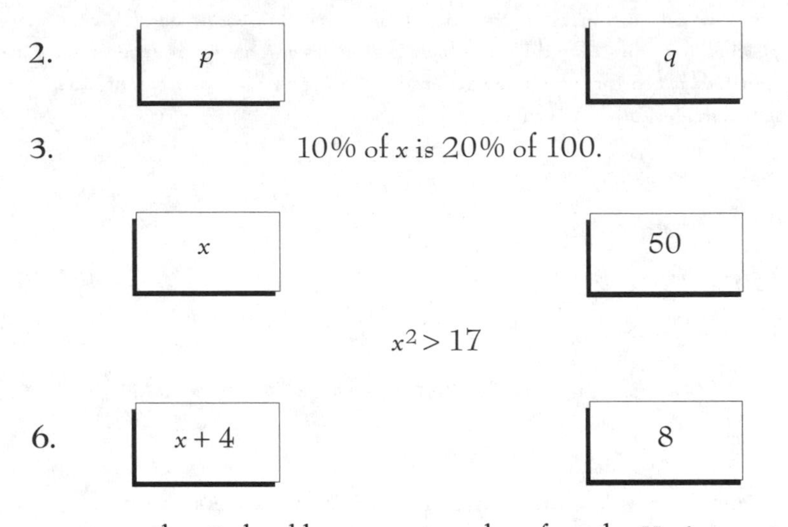

The answer to number 2 should not require a lot of math. You've got two numbers and their average is 3—try plugging in $p = 2$ and $q = 4$, and then $p = 4$ and $q = 2$. Either could work. Can you tell whether p or q is bigger? No. Your answer is D.

How about number 3? 10% of x = 20% of 100, or 20. If 10% of x is 20, x is a whole lot bigger than 50. The answer is A.

Do you see how you don't really need to do much math? Work smart on these easy quant comps; it will give you more time for the tricky ones coming up.

Number 6 is a slightly harder problem (it's the first of the medium questions). Did you catch the trick? Let's look at it:

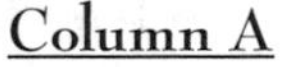

Column B

$x + 4$	8

Before you do anything, write down "A B C D" and get ready to POE. You'll need to plug in for x so that $x^2 > 17$ (that must be true). Why do you think column A is $x + 4$ and column B is 8? Because the test writer wants you to make them equal. Put in 4 for x. Is $4^2 > 17$? No, so 4 is too small. x must be bigger than 4, which makes column A bigger. Is (A) the answer? Not necessarily.

Once you show that column A is bigger one time, cross off B and C. (Column B cannot always, always be bigger if column A is bigger once, and the two columns cannot always, always be equal if column A is bigger once.) Now let's look again. Are there any weird numbers (0, 1, negatives, fractions) you can plug into $x^2 > 17$ to make it true? What happens when you square a negative number? It becomes positive. So x could be 5, but it could also be –5. If x is –5, then column B is bigger. The answer is D.

As you can see, POE was essential on even a number 6 quant comp. Don't let the fact that the answer choices aren't printed for you keep you from using POE. For every medium and difficult quant comp question, jot down a quick "A B C D." Then, as you "solve" the problem the first time, get rid of two answer choices. If you had no idea what else to do, you would still have a fifty-fifty shot at guessing the right answer. Now try some harder quant comps. Use lots of POE, lots of smart guessing, and as little math as possible:

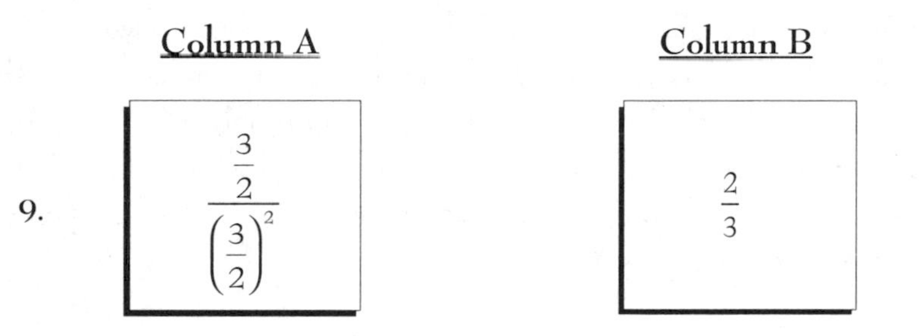

First, look at number 9. As soon as you wrote "A B C D" you should have crossed off D—there are no variables in this problem, so it has to have an answer. Next, because you are comparing and not calculating, work smart by simplifying column A:

$$\frac{\left(\frac{3}{2}\right)(1)}{\left(\frac{3}{2}\right)\left(\frac{3}{2}\right)} = \frac{(1)}{\left(\frac{3}{2}\right)}$$

Then flip to simplify, and you have $\frac{2}{3}$ in column A. The answer is C.

On questions like this, do as little math as possible (like not taking the time to square $\frac{3}{2}$). Do just enough so that you can see the answer.

Did you work smart on number 14? I know you wrote down "A B C D" before you did anything else. What do you think Jane is picking on this one? B, of course—she thinks $(x + 1)^2$ must be bigger than x^2. Since this is a number 14 out of 15, there is no way the answer is B, so cross it off. (If you picked B, don't feel bad—that's what Thelma wanted you to do.) Next, solve the problem first by plugging in an easy number like 2.

Plugging in 2 immediately eliminates A and C, and since B is already gone, the answer must be D.

I know, I know, this is exactly the kind of "do no math" problem that drives you crazy. POE says it's (D), but why is it (D)? To satisfy your need to know why the answer is (D), and to convince you to trust POE, let's do the rest of the problem. Plug in a weird number for x, like -2. $-2^2 = 4$ and $(-2 + 1)^2 = 1$. This time column A is bigger, and since we already know that when $x = 2$, column B is bigger, then the answer must be D—which you already knew.

Working out the rest of a problem while you're practicing is okay if you need that extra reinforcement. Remember, however, that you learned about the structure of the test and about Jane Bloggs answers so that you can work smart on problems, use POE, and guess the right answer without investing too much time and energy. Don't expend energy where it's not needed—solving a problem by working smart puts you more in control of your test than grinding your way to each answer.

GUESS SMART

For a little more guessing practice, try to guess smart on the following math problems. Use POE to narrow your choices, then take a guess at each one (go ahead—there's no risk here). For each answer you cross off, note your reasoning.

24. There are 125 students enrolled at the Language Academy. 40 students take German, 80 students take Spanish, and 35 students take Latin. If none of the students who take Latin take any other language, what percent of the students taking German are also taking Spanish?

    (A) 30
    (B) 37.5
    (C) 40
    (D) 75
    (E) 80

How'd it go? Check your work against mine to see if you guessed smart:

24. There are 125 students enrolled at the Language Academy. 40 students take German, 80 students take Spanish, and 35 students take Latin. STOP!

So there are 125 students taking classes... no, wait, if you add the numbers, there are 155 students taking classes... I'm so confused... What's the deal with those extra 30 students?

If none of the students who take Latin take any other language, what percent of the students taking German are also taking Spanish?

~~(A)~~	30	Jane answer—I can get this number by adding up number of students in the classes and subtracting 125. Too obvious.
(B)	37.5	a smart guess
~~(C)~~	40	Worse than Jane—the number of students taking German
(D)	75	a smart guess
~~(E)~~	80	Worse than Jane—the number of students taking Spanish

The smart guesses here are (B) or (D). You should have gotten rid of (C) and (E), since those are numbers in the problem, and (A) 30 was too easy a number to come up with. If you guessed either (B) or (D), you guessed smart. (The answer is D).

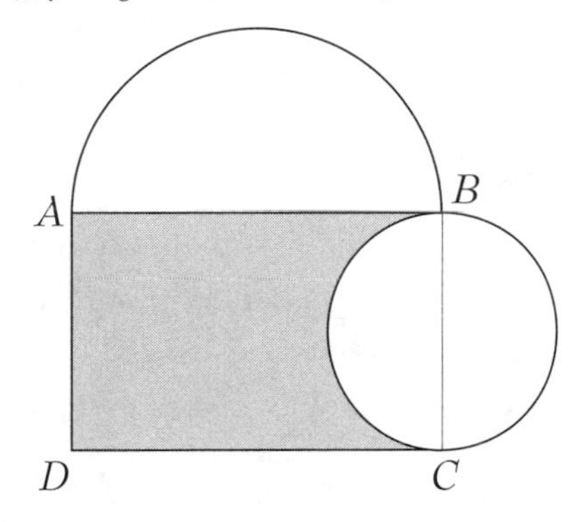

22. In the figure above, if the semicircle arc AB has length 6π and the circumference of the circle with diameter BC is 8π, what is the area of the shaded region?

    (A) $12 - 4\pi$
    (B) $24 - 8\pi$
    (C) $48 - 8\pi$
    (D) $96 - 8\pi$
    (E) $96 - 16\pi$

Whoa, I have no idea how to do this. Area of the shaded region... Let me get rid of bad answers first...

~~(A)~~ $12 - 4\pi$ π is a little more than 3, so this is a negative number

~~(B)~~ $24 - 8\pi$ ditto

(C) $48 - 8\pi$ 48 – 24ish = 24ish

(D) $96 - 8\pi$ 96 – 24ish = 72ish

(E) $96 - 16\pi$ 96 – 48ish = 48ish

The smart guesses here are (C), (D), or (E). (A) and (B) are negative numbers. If you have no idea how to do this problem, take a smart guess. To take a smarter guess, look at the shaded region. Does it look like half or more than half? Since the diagram is drawn to scale, and the shaded region looks like more than half the rectangle, the only answer that represents "more than half" is (D).

How did you do? If you didn't guess as smart as you would have liked, don't worry—that's why you're practicing. But even if you just got rid of a few of the blatantly wrong answers for the right reasons, you're well on your way to consistently guessing smart. If you narrowed the answer down to the two smartest guesses and then guessed the wrong one, you're still guessing smart—every time you get rid of wrong answer choices, you increase your odds of guessing smart and getting a higher score.

Guess Smart in Verbal, Too

Now let's do a little smart guessing in Verbal. The main stumbling block in both Sentence Completions and Analogies is vocabulary. Therefore, here are some harder sentence completion and analogy questions with some missing words to represent words you might not know on the test. Use the information you have, work smart, POE, and then guess smart.

9. Most of Rick's friends think his life is incredibly ______, but sadly he spends most of his time in ______activities.

   (A) fruitful . . productive
   (B) ???? . . ????
   (C) ???? . . mundane
   (D) varied . . sportive
   (E) ???? . . luxurious

For this sentence, it may be hard to come up with exact words, but it shouldn't be hard to tell whether the author wants positive or negative words in the blanks. Rick *sadly* spends most of his time doing some negative activities. The word *but* tells you that his friends think the opposite of him, so the first blank needs to be a more positive word.

Check the second words first (looking for a negative word):

(A) Is *productive* a negative word? No, cross it off.

(B) You don't know the second word here, so keep it.

(C) Is *mundane* a negative word? Sure is—mundane, boring. Keep it.

(D) Is *sportive* a negative word? Doesn't sound like one. This is also very Jane—sportive activities. Cross this off.

(E) Is *luxurious* a negative word? No, so cross this off.

You have (B) and (C) left, and you don't know either of the first words, so take a guess—either guess is a smart one.

Now try some analogies. Make a sentence if you can, then use POE by filling in the words you do know to see if they are possible. Cross off Jane answers and remember that hard questions typically have hard answers. If you can't make a sentence of the stem words, see if you can make a clear, defining sentence of each answer choice. If not, cross it off.

20. ADDENDUM : BOOK ::

(A) signature : letter
(B) ???? : symphony
(C) ???? : will
(D) heading : folder
(E) footnote : story

23. ???? : ???? ::

(A) dither : choice
(B) dawdle : excuse
(C) chatter : speech
(D) mope : laughter
(E) bustle : arrival

How did you do on question 20? "Addendum is something that is added on to a book." What's Jane picking? (E), so cross it off. Let's check the others:

(A) Is a *signature* something that is added on to a *letter*? Sort of, but not in the same way, plus this is way too easy for a question 20. Cross it off.

(B) Is there something that can be added onto a *symphony*? Sounds possible. Keep it.

(C) Is there something that can be added onto a *will*? Probably. Keep it.

(D) Is a *heading* something that is added onto a *folder*? Not really, cross it off.

You've narrowed it down to (B) and (C). Both are good, smart guesses, so pick one and move on!

How did you solve number 23? It is doable, you just need to go straight to those answer choices:

(A) Can you make a clear, defining sentence with *dither* and *choice*? Only if you know what *dither* means. Leave it for now.

(B) Can you make a clear, defining sentence with *dawdle* and *excuse*? Not if you're not sure of what *dawdle* means. Keep it.

(C) Can you make a clear, defining sentence with *chatter* and *speech*? Sure: Chatter is a rapid, incessant form of speech. Keep it.

(D) Can you make a clear, defining sentence with *mope* and *laughter*? Not really. Cross it out.

(E) Can you make a clear, defining sentence with *bustle* and *arrival*? Well, *bustle* means lots of activity, which might take place at some arrivals, but I would bet you wouldn't find the word *arrival* under the definition of *bustle*. Cross it off.

You are left with (A), (B) and (C). Let's guess smart. You have no idea what the given words are, but you do know that this is a very hard question. What are your smart guesses, given that hard questions typically have hard answers? (A) or (B). While (C), *chatter* and *speech*, is a decent choice, the words aren't really hard enough words for a number 23. In any case, by eliminating answer choices, you've significantly improved your odds of getting the question right.

ARE YOU SAT-SMART YET?

You've just worked through a whole chapter designed to make you more confident about working smart (cutting the right corners) and guessing smart (using POE and guessing assertively). Did it work? Do you need more practice? Here are some ideas for drills to help you hone your work smart and guess smart skills. As you do these drills either on your own or with a study partner, remember

- only do as much work as you need to
- easy questions have easy answers, medium questions have answers that are slightly harder and may contain tricks and traps, and hard questions typically have hard answers (and definitely contain tricks and traps)
- use POE to get rid of obviously wrong answer choices
- four out of five answer choices are wrong
- assume every answer is wrong until proven right
- as you practice, circle or underline what makes each answer choice wrong—then cross the choice off
- if you get rid of even one answer choice, take a smart guess

Work Smart, Guess Smart Drills

Write Your Own Bad Answers. Think like Thelma and create your own SAT questions and answers. Be sure to think up some good trap answers and a clear right answer. Work with your study partner to make up the questions and answers, or make up your own while she makes up hers, and then the two of you can exchange questions and evaluate. To make math questions, take questions from a Grid-In section in *10 Real SATs*, and make them into multiple-choice questions by writing in the right answer plus four Thelma-style wrong answer choices. Use your Vocabulary Stash to create analogies and sentence completions. If you want to do a few critical reading questions, take an existing passage and write your own questions and answers for it.

Teach Me Why It's Wrong. Being able to explain why wrong answers are wrong is the best way to sharpen your ability to identify bad answer choices. Choose a section or set of questions to annotate. Do the problems, find the right answer, and indicate why each wrong answer is wrong. Then, teach the problems to your study partner. You can also teach each other after doing timed sections or a full-length test. Check your sections together. Whenever your partner gets a question wrong, you play the teacher and explain it to her. Let her do the same for you. If you both missed a problem, work together to figure out what you both did wrong.

One-to-One Drill. Choose a set of questions to do, and give yourself only one minute per question. If, for example, you want to do 12 quant comp problems, allow yourself only 12 minutes. This increased time pressure will force you to work smarter and guess smarter. Once you've finished doing the set under timed conditions, take as much time as you want to rework the same set of questions with a different-colored pen before you check the answers. How many answers would you change? Did you make any Jane guesses the first time through? Were most of your guesses smart guesses? Try this drill on both Math and Verbal questions.

Quiz Time. Make up a verbal quiz for your study partner and have her make up one for you. Put together a short set of analogies or sentence completions, leaving out some of the words. Or select a set of critical reading questions to do, with the line references and the blurb, not the passage. Quiz each other and then go over your guessing strategies together.

Quant Comp POE Drill. Do a quant comp section by working smart. Write down "A B C D" for each of the medium and hard problems, then only do the amount of math you need to do to figure out which column is bigger. Have your partner check your work to see if you did more math than you needed to. Do the same for her.

Chapter 9
CONCENTRATE

SOLUTION #6: CONCENTRATE

As you know, concentrating on the SAT is of paramount importance. But concentrating intensely for three hours is tough. And girls, more often than boys, complain that they are distracted during the SAT by things going on around them, lingering worries over specific questions, or overall test anxiety. These distractions tend to fall into one of three categories—worry about others, worry about self, or worry about the test.

WHAT CAN YOU DO?

As a manager at The Princeton Review, I used to gather together my colleagues at the beginning of every week. For some reason, I was in the habit of starting each meeting by saying, "Okay, these are the things we need to worry about this week." My colleague and good friend Debbie always smiled and replied, "Why don't we just do something about them instead of worrying?" Debbie, of course, was right. Worrying about things—such as what you need to do this week, how much time you have left on a section, or what the tester next to you is doing—does you no good. Doing something about the things that are within your control and letting go of the things that are not will remove the worry and the distraction. This chapter will teach you to improve your ability to concentrate on the SAT by

- creating your own personal testing space
- preventing the distractions you can prevent and coping with the ones you can't
- using focusing techniques designed to increase your ability to concentrate

CREATE YOUR PERSONAL TESTING SPACE

Meditation instructors often tell you to designate a specific place in your house as your meditation spot. When you create a place in which the only thing you do is meditate, you train your brain not to be distracted when you're in that place.

ENTER YOUR SPACE

You can do the same thing with the SAT. Although you obviously can't choose where you're taking the test, you can create your own personal testing space, both during the test itself and during your practice sessions. Before you do any timed practice, take a moment to put a box around your work space. Hold your arms out in front of you, spaced just a little wider than your body, and then lay them on your desk or work space. Make sure your practice materials fit within the space your arms have created. If you're having trouble visualizing your box, use tape to mark the corners of your work space and practice a few times within that space. Then remove the tape but continue to picture those corners in your mind. On test day, as soon as you're seated, create your personal space. Outline your space with your arms. After a moment, remove your arms but imagine that your testing boundaries are still in place. Focus yourself, and make sure your testing materials and your answer sheet fit in the space. If you become distracted during the test, sit up straight and use your arms to quickly recreate your boundaries. Refocus yourself and continue working.

CENTER YOURSELF IN YOUR SPACE

Every time you enter your personal testing space, focus your mind before you do any work. Take a few deep breaths. As you breathe in, tell yourself, "I am focused," or, "I am now ready for the SAT." As you breathe out, empty your mind of other thoughts.

RETURN TO YOUR SPACE

If you become distracted during the test, take a moment to re-center yourself. Recreate your boundaries with your arms, then take a few deep breaths and repeat to yourself: "I am focused," or, "I am again ready for the SAT." Continually bring yourself back into your testing space. Practice this at home, so that by test day it's second nature.

You Can Start Now

In my husband's graduate program, a classmate would spend thirty seconds or so doing deep breathing exercises before starting every exam. At first the other students were unnerved by this—Why isn't this guy starting the test? Doesn't he know he's wasting precious time? A few of the other students finally decided to join him and afterward noticed how much calmer they felt during the test and how much easier it was for them to focus. After a while, the entire class was taking a thirty-second pause before beginning each exam. And, according to the instructor, it must have been doing something, because their exam grades began to improve. The moral of the story: If you need a break, take it.

NO MORE DISTRACTIONS FROM OTHERS

If you tend to be distracted by your environment or the people around you, you need to learn how to prevent the distractions you can control and prepare yourself for the distractions you can't control. Being able to put a wall between you and external distractions will help you immeasurably during the SAT, so be sure to practice creating your personal testing space beforehand. In addition to practicing at home, you may want to create your personal space at school. Try it during a test. Then try it when there's some background noise, like the marching band outside the window. Finally, try to create your personal space in a busy place, like the cafeteria. The better you get at creating your personal space, the less distracted you will be by those around you on test day.

Some external distractions are within your control and can be prevented or at least diffused. For example, if you can't stand to hear unprepared testers ask around for a pencil, you can bring some extras to share. If it's important to you to test at a particular test center, register early so that you don't get shut out of that site. And if you won't be able to concentrate if you sit by the window, tell the proctor beforehand that you'd like to sit somewhere else. You may not have a say in this, but then again you might. You'll never know unless you ask.

WHERE TO TEST

Choose a testing environment that will contain the fewest number of distractions for you. For example, if sitting next to so-and-so or being near *her* will drive you crazy, you may wish to test somewhere other than your school. On the other hand, you may be the kind of person who feels much more comfortable in familiar surroundings; you may want to be able to put your coat in your locker and talk to a few friends before the test starts. Where you test is your choice—as long as you register early. Some students actually prefer testing in an unfamiliar environment. They're less concerned about those around them, and they're able to take the test more seriously. If you want to test somewhere other than your school but don't want to go alone, see if your study partner wants to join you.

> Rebecca, 18
>
> "Taking this test in the environment of my high school cafeteria was too relaxed and was reflected in my score. I did better in another school environment."

NO MORE DISTRACTIONS FROM YOURSELF

Many personal worries are well within your control. Consider first what causes you to worry.

WHAT TO WEAR

For example, if you absolutely hate to be cold, being cold during the SAT will challenge your ability to concentrate. Bring a sweater, or dress in layers so you'll be comfortable. Clothes in general can definitely influence the way you test. Some people like to "dress for success" when they take a test, while others only feel ready to get down to work when they're in jeans and a T-shirt. In any case, you should definitely wear comfortable clothing—after all, you have to sit at a desk for three hours straight; tight jeans will get old after a while.

TO EAT OR NOT TO EAT

Some of us don't like to eat much in the morning, especially if we're a little nervous. However, the SAT is a long test, and your brain will burn up a lot of calories, even though you're just sitting for three hours. Even if you're not a breakfast-eater, or not a morning person at all, find something to eat beforehand that's high in protein—it takes the body longer to burn protein than anything else, and eating protein before the test will prevent that late-morning crash that can come from eating lots of bread and sugar first thing. If you can't imagine going three hours without food, pack an energy bar and a bottle of water in your bag. You probably can't eat in the testing room, but you should be able to grab a quick drink and a snack in the hallway at break. If you know you'll need to eat, find out the policy at your test site before you get there so you can figure out how to grab a quick pick-me-up when you need it.

ASK FOR WHAT YOU NEED

If you need something during the test, or if something is really distracting you, don't hesitate to speak up. If an oscillating fan keeps blowing your answer sheet onto the floor, ask to have the fan moved or turned off. If you're left-handed but get seated at a right-handed desk, ask to be moved. If you're working at a long table and the guy next to you keeps bouncing his leg and shaking the table, speak to him during the break, or ask to be moved. Don't just endure a distraction and hope that it won't affect your score; speak up for yourself and try to get the help you need. You are the only one who will look out for your best interests.

NO MORE DISTRACTIONS FROM THE TEST

TALK YOUR WAY THROUGH IT

During tests, some of us are plagued by those continuous running monologues: "Will I be able to finish before time is called?" "I hope I did all right on that last section." "I picked (B) on that question, but maybe it's (D). Should I go back to that one again?" If this happens to you, replace your unproductive monologue with one that will increase your focus:

Here we go, math. Now I'm on question one and I'm gonna kick butt. Okay, add that... got it... Yes, it's (A). I rock at math. Now, on to question two. Easy, no problem... write it out, carry the two... it's (B). Two down, baby, we're cruisin'...all right, next one... read it, think it through...that's what they want... cross off (A), (B) is out, (C) okay, (D) out, (E) nope... it's (C). Ha, do no math and get the answer! Doin' great, let's keep going...

By creating a running monologue that's totally focused on what you're doing, your brain has no room for distracting thoughts. Notice, too, that this monologue provides constant reinforcement and continuous encouragement. This is especially important when you are on sections that intimidate you. If you hit something difficult, talk your way through that, too:

Okay, this one's tough—I know that word but it's not coming to me. Well, let's get rid of answer choices. It can't be (A) and... it can't be (E) or (D). Okay, guess between (B) and (C)... I pick... (C). It's a smart guess, and I'm gonna move on....

You do your best, you stay focused, you move on. You do not beat yourself up while you're testing. Never say to yourself, "I should have studied more vocabulary," "I wish I had done more timed work," etc. Comments like that are not useful during the test. Your monologue should keep your techniques and strategies at hand, plus act as a constant reminder that you're doing your best. Practice creating a positive, focusing monologue for yourself while you do the following problem:

21. If $x^2 = 16$ and $y^2 = 4$, what is the greatest possible value of $(x - y)^2$?

Did your monologue sound something like this?

Alright, number 21 grid-in... "If $x^2 = 16$ and $y^2 = 4$, what is the greatest possible value of $(x - y)^2$?" Greatest possible value... that means y needs to be as small as possible, and x needs to be as big as possible... I'm onto you, Thelma. Since we're squaring, y can be negative...-2. x can be 4. I'm all over this. $4 - (-2)$ is the same as $4 + 2$ baby, and $6^2 = 36$. Grid it in and we are on our way. I am getting so good at this stuff...

Try one more before moving on. Make sure your brain isn't wandering off course—use your monologue to stay focused:

8. Since many disadvantaged individuals view their situations as ______ as well as intolerable, their attitudes are best described as ______ .

(A) squalid. .obscure
(B) unpleasant. .bellicose
(C) acute. .sanguine
(D) immutable. .resigned
(E) political. .perplexed

Did you stay focused the whole time? How did you do? Here's my monologue:

> I am rockin' on sentence comps; only two to go in this set. Bring it on... "Since many disadvantaged individuals view their situations as blank as well as intolerable, their attitudes are best described as blank." Let's try the second blank. Second blank is talking about the attitude of disadvantaged individuals, and the sentence already says they view their situation as intolerable, so the second blank must also be negative. Check the second words of each choice...(A) obscure means unknown or hidden—that's doesn't make sense, so cross it off. I don't know the words in (B) or (C) so keep them. (D) resigned is kinda negative, so keep it. (E) perplexed would mean the individuals are confused, but the sentence doesn't say that—cross it off. This is tricky, but I'll figure it out. Okay, first blank. First blank is talking about the situation of disadvantaged individuals. The clue says it's intolerable, so whatever's happening, it's also somehow negative. (B) unpleasant is negative, but it's a very easy word for a number 8, so I'll make it my last guess. (C) acute doesn't work, so I'll cross it off. (D) immutable is a hard word that I don't know. (B) and (D) are the best choices here. I'll guess (D)...It's a smart guess, and it's time to move on. I've only got one more sentence comp to go...

You get the idea. Talking your way through each problem keeps your mind busy and focused—exactly what it needs to be so that it doesn't begin to wander or worry. It also keeps you in control of the test by keeping your mind in work mode. You're not passively reading and then trying a few things; you're working each problem, focusing on important information, and getting rid of minutiae (minor details—stash the word if you didn't know it). Practice talking your way through some timed sections to see if it helps you maintain your focus. The more you talk, the better you'll get at it.

DETAILS, DETAILS

We females often have an eye for details, which is partly why we're so successful in school. However, some details on the SAT are designed to distract you. How do you know when to pay attention to details on the SAT versus when to ignore them?

Remember these guidelines:

- **Don't read to learn.** The sole purpose of taking the SAT is to score as high as you can. Don't get bogged down by (or too interested in) the content of a critical reading passage. It may be on a topic that interests you, but this is not the time to learn about that topic. Make a mental note that you want to read up on Katherine Mansfield (or whomever), and then get focused on reading only the details you need to answer the questions on the test.

- **Read what you need when you need it.** As you learned in the verbal chapter, it's best not to focus on any detail in a reading passage until you know you need it to answer a question. On some critical reading passages there are whole paragraphs for which there are no questions. If you spend your time and energy reading those paragraphs, you will lose time you could use to answer questions. Only read for details once you know you need them.
- **A little detail goes a long way.** When you do need to read for details, break the passage or the question into manageable pieces. The answer can often be found in just a few words. Use your pencil to cross off irrelevant portions of a question, and circle or underline important phrases. Try it on the following word problem:

HERB PRICES OF DISTRIBUTOR X

Spice	Price Per Pound
basil	$6.00
parsley	$4.00
rosemary	$8.00
thyme	$7.00

The owner of an herb store buys 2 pounds each of dried basil, parsley, rosemary, and thyme from Distributor X. She then sells all the herbs at $2.00 per ounce. What, in dollars, is her total profit (1 pound = 16 ounces)?

How did you do? There are a lot of details in this problem, some important, some redundant. After you "edit" the question, it should look something like the problem on the top of the next page.

HERB PRICES OF DISTRIBUTOR X

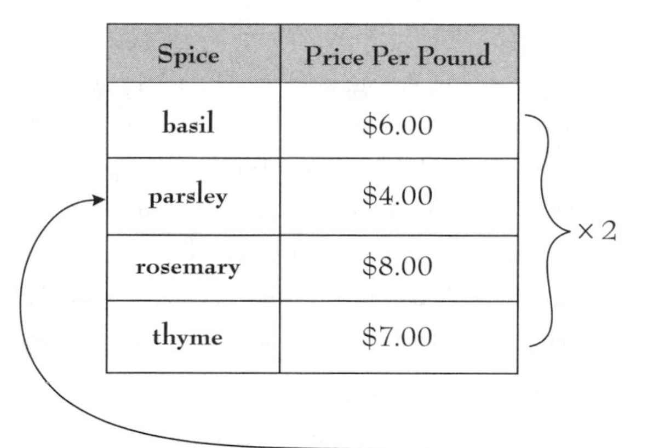

Spice	Price Per Pound
basil	$6.00
parsley	$4.00
rosemary	$8.00
thyme	$7.00

The owner of an herb store buys 2 pounds each of ~~dried basil, parsley, rosemary, and thyme from Distributor X~~. She then sells all of the herbs at $2.00 per ounce. What, in dollars, is her total profit (1 pound = 16 ounces)?

The details that matter in this problem are that she bought two pounds of each herb and sold each herb for $2.00 per ounce. Also, you need to know that there are 16 ounces in a pound and that the question part of the question wants to know her total profit. Repeating the names of the herbs is redundant, and knowing whom she bought them from is irrelevant. (The answer is $206, by the way.)

- **What's in a name?** On the SAT, not much. Other than keeping track of who's who in a word problem, the names used on the SAT are, for the most part, irrelevant. And in some cases, they may distract you from what you're working on. When you encounter names you find awkward, difficult, or simply annoying, cross them out and replace them with letters, names of your choosing, or pronouns such as "she." In fact, adding a few more female characters to the SAT can only help. Just don't get bogged down in details.

Write It Down

As I've mentioned several times, writing is one of the best ways to focus, and it's essential on the SAT. Writing is also something at which girls excel. When I teach an SAT course, I often have to push my male students to write things down, while my female students seem to know the importance of writing right from the start. Writing will not only help you solve questions accurately and effectively, but it will also keep your mind from meandering from the SAT.

WHAT TO WRITE

Here are some general guidelines for writing on the SAT:

- **Write on, write on.** As you know, your SAT test booklet is yours. You're allowed to write anywhere in the booklet you wish. Don't feel that this is a textbook that you can't mark up. Cross out irrelevant stuff, underline or circle important information, and write down the words or numbers you need to solve each problem quickly and accurately. Also, before you begin a particular question type, like quant comp or analogies, you might want to make a quick note of the steps you want to remember. The more you write, the more focused you'll be.
- **Cross it off.** When evaluating answer choices, cross off the ones you think are wrong—and remember, four out of every five answer choices are wrong, so you should be doing lots of crossing off.
- **Circle your answers.** When you choose your answer to a question, circle it in your test booklet. Then transfer your answers to the answer sheet in blocks. On the regular Math sections, transfer answers one page at a time. On the Quant Comp and Grid-In sections, transfer answers by question type. In Verbal, transfer your answers at the end of Sentence Completions, and then again at the end of Analogies. You can do critical reading questions the same way. Just be sure that time isn't called before you transfer your answers! Transferring answers in blocks keeps you from going back and forth between the test and your answer sheet on every question. Once you near the five-minute mark in each section, make sure you transfer all of your answers to the answer sheet.
- **Write for you.** You are the only one who will ever see what you write in your test booklet. ETS will not read it, so relax. If you need to write down "3 + 5 = 8" because you're blanking out, then write it down.

DON'T GET CARRIED AWAY

Of course, you don't want to spend so much of your time writing that you're not spending enough time answering questions. You need to know what's important to write down and what's not. Practice focus-writing while you take a timed practice section to see how much writing you need to do to keep your mind on task.

Back into Focus

The SAT is a long test, and chances are that at some point in the middle of it you're going to get distracted, tired, or unfocused. No problem. You simply need to go into the test with some refocusing techniques that will help you "rein in your brain" when it decides to wander off. You can prevent a fair amount of mind-meandering by just using your breaks wisely. Are you the type of person who hates to sit for three hours? Get up, stretch, and walk around during your breaks. If you're more the kind of person who needs a little down time every couple of hours, use your breaks to go inside—close your eyes, take a few deep breaths, and try to relax for a minute. While you practice full-length tests at home, note when you begin to get tired or lose focus; are you close to break time? If so, great. Plan in advance what you will do during your break to give your brain the boost it needs to make it to the end of the test.

Try Some of These

Here are some ways you can get yourself focused before the test, during each section, and during your breaks. Consider each strategy, then try some out as you practice to see how they work. In addition, develop some focusing techniques of your own.

My Pretest Focusing Strategies

To help me focus before the start of the test, I want to

- ☐ create my personal testing space
- ☐ do some deep breathing. Oxygen stimulates the brain and calms the body.
- ☐ drink some water so I don't get thirsty (not too much water—you don't want to be distracted by the need for a bathroom break!)
- ☐ sit down with my eyes closed and picture myself doing well on the test
- ☐ do some easy practice problems to warm up (if your proctor lets you bring practice material to your desk)
- ☐ Write your own strategy here: ______________________________

____

____

____

____

☐ Write your own strategy here: ____________________

____

____

____

____

My Breaktime Refocusing Strategies

To help me refocus during my breaks, I want to

- ☐ stand up and stretch to get my body moving and blood circulating
- ☐ team up with a friend and take turns giving each other a shoulder massage
- ☐ eat an energy bar or get a quick drink of water to revitalize myself
- ☐ walk around the room to get my blood flowing
- ☐ go to the bathroom
- ☐ do some deep breathing to help clear my mind of the sections I've just completed
- ☐ energize my brain through laughing, humming, or vocalizing (The brain is fed by sounds from the environment. Since you can't put your Walkman on, hum a little song to yourself or laugh out loud.)
- ☐ recreate my personal test space just before beginning the next section
- ☐ Write your own strategy here: ____________________

  ____

  ____

  ____

  ____

- ☐ Write your own strategy here: ____________________

  ____

  ____

  ____

  ____

My Mid-Section Refocusing Strategies

To help me refocus if I start to drift during a section, I want to

- ☐ write a note in my test, such as "stay focused" or "concentrate"
- ☐ do "bubble breathing"—while bubbling in a set of answers, breathe deeply in and out to get ready for the next set
- ☐ do a quick meditation—stop, put my pencil down, close my eyes, and breathe deeply in and out. While breathing, think something positive, such as "I can focus," "I am doing well," or "I am the testing queen." Breathe in and out three times or so. Then finish with a deep breath, open my eyes, grab my pencil, and go.
- ☐ smile or laugh about one of the silly questions or about how insane all this pressure is, and try to think of the SAT as a game rather than a stressful exam
- ☐ Write your own strategy here: ____________________

  ____

  ____

  ____

  ____
- ☐ Write your own strategy here: ____________________

  ____

  ____

  ____

  ____

Don't Be Lost, Late, or Lacking

Abide by these simple don'ts to avoid unnecessary stress on SAT day:

- **Don't get lost.** If you're going to a test site that you have never been to before, take a drive there the week before the test. And don't just drive by the building! Park your car so you know where to park, and then go inside the building if you can. See if you can find out exactly where the test will be held and what door to enter through the morning of the test. All these steps will save you time and prevent potential stress on the morning of the exam.

- **Don't be late.** Being late can cause all kinds of stress, and you could be barred from taking the test if you don't arrive on time. If you tend to be late, do what you need to do so that you're not late that morning. Get all your stuff together the night before, including your clothes for the next day. Make sure someone else in your house knows what time you have to wake up. If you're not a morning person, make yourself get up early every day during the week or so that leads up to the test. Shift your body schedule in advance so that SAT morning isn't a shock to your system.
- **Don't be lacking.** There are certain things you must bring to the SAT, and other things that you'll really want to have with you. First, you cannot get into the testing center without your admission ticket and a picture ID. Don't forget them. In addition, you'll need at least two sharpened number two pencils, a watch, and a calculator. You may also want to bring a snack, a drink, a sweater, and some warm-up questions. If there's anything else you might need, such as tampons or tissues, be sure to bring that, too. Chapter 11 contains your Test Day Checklist. Go through it the week before the SAT and gather together everything you'll need for SAT morning. In addition, plan to recheck your Test Day Checklist the morning of the test to make sure you don't forget anything.

Chapter 10
Be a Little Nervous

SOLUTION #7: BE A LITTLE NERVOUS

First off, I think it's safe to say that you're probably less nervous about the SAT now than you were before you started reading this book. Understanding the gender gap problem and the solutions to it has hopefully assuaged (great SAT word—look it up and stash it if you don't know it) some of your fears. Learning each solution, mastering each technique, and practicing under timed conditions will leave you in control of the SAT.

I KNOW, BUT...

Are you the type of person who gets nervous even when you're totally prepared? This happens to lots of people. The important thing is to understand yourself. What kinds of activities make you nervous? For each of the following, check the column that applies to you:

	Does not make me nervous	*Makes me a little nervous*	*Makes me way nervous*
A major competition, meet, or game	______	______	______
A big exam	______	______	______
The SAT	______	______	______
Going out on stage	______	______	______
Speaking in public	______	______	______
A roller coaster	______	______	______
A college interview	______	______	______
A job interview	______	______	______
Asking for the car keys...again	______	______	______

Even *She* Gets Nervous

While not everyone gets nervous about the same things, even the most confident among us experiences an occasional jitter here and there. But high performers have a way of controlling their nerves. Have you caught glimpses of Michelle Kwan as she visualizes her entire routine before going out on the ice? Or what about Venus Williams on the sidelines before the final match at Wimbledon? She seems completely unaware of the crowd around her; she's totally focused inward as she gets ready for the match. These famous women are preparing themselves for a major undertaking by getting psyched—channeling their nervous energy so that it will help them perform their best. They know that, if channeled properly, adrenaline will help them. Adrenaline makes us feel on...alert, focused, full of energy, ready to act. That's exactly the way you want to feel when you take the SAT.

Just a Little, Please

While adrenaline can be beneficial, it has its negative side, too. Too much adrenaline or nervous energy can be distracting. For some people, being nervous is the only thing they can think about, and that problem feeds on itself—they can't stop thinking about being nervous, which just makes them feel more nervous. This type of nervous energy—anxiety—makes them feel powerless or out of control. Anxiety is not useful because it makes it hard to concentrate and undermines your self-confidence. How can you maintain a healthy amount of nervous energy without becoming anxious? By getting psyched—channeling your nervous energy. Solution #7: Be A Little Nervous will teach you to channel your nervous energy with

- exercises designed to help you get psyched for the SAT
- on-the-spot statements to help you to maintain your self-confidence and control over the test
- games and activities to help prevent yourself from taking the test too seriously
- ten-second tension relievers to do at any time during the test

Get Psyched

First, a story. When I was in college, I did a lot of theater. My first role was in a very funny play called *A Bad Year for Tomatoes.* I wasn't cast in the play initially, but two weeks before the show, the lead quit, and the director turned to me. "Can you do it?" she asked. What could I say? I spent the next two weeks eating, sleeping, and breathing *A Bad Year for Tomatoes.* I was so busy learning my lines that I forgot about being nervous—until opening night, of course. As I showered just before the performance, I tried to calm myself down: *Everything will be fine... you know your lines... you can do it...it doesn't matter how you feel... there's no way out... you can't let everybody down....* It wasn't working. Then I decided to try something else: I closed my eyes and pictured myself at my best. I thought back to times in which I had felt great about myself—my high school graduation, the day I learned how to sail, the last time I'd made all my friends laugh, and so on. I pictured myself during those moments, and pretty soon I began to relax. *I was pretty funny that time... I felt so good when my hard work paid off... I really liked leading that group.* Next, I tried carrying those feelings to the present: *I am confident... I am good at what I do... I feel good about myself.* Once I felt grounded, I began to apply those affirmations to the evening's performance: *I will be great in this show... I know my stuff... people will enjoy my performance.* After a while, I felt ready for the show—and was impeccably clean after a long shower. When the curtain went up that night, I was ready. The performance went off without a hitch.

You Be the Star

Getting psyched for something important—like going out on stage, playing a big match, or taking the SAT—begins by reminding yourself of how you've succeeded in the past. Refueling your self-confidence with good memories will allow you to transfer those feelings to what you're about to do. Use the Get Psyched Worksheet to help you get psyched before and during the SAT.

GET-PSYCHED WORKSHEET

At my best in the past . . .

Describe one or two situations in which you were at your best—feeling on top of the world, invincible, excellent

Focus on the feelings you had. Write down some words or phrases to describe how you felt at the time. Example: *I felt in control, I was confident*

At my best today . . .

Now use those phrases to describe yourself in the present tense: *I am in control, I am confident*

Use your affirmations to describe yourself in relation to the SAT: *I am in control of the SAT, I feel secure about the SAT*

FEEL GOOD ON THE SPOT

I AM THE TESTING QUEEN

Another way to get psyched is to use positive affirmations—statements that make you feel good immediately and remind you that you're in control. Affirmations simply are words or phrases of praise and encouragement. Here are some examples of affirmations you can use on the spot:

Affirmation	What it's good for
I rock at math *or* I *know* math techniques	*Reinforces confidence during the Math section*
You can't outwit me, Thelma *or* I'm on to you, Thelma *or* What are you trying to pull, Thelma?	*Bolsters confidence when faced with challenging problems*
I am totally prepared *or* I am the SAT Queen	*Quells feelings of insecurity before or during each section*
My vocabulary is vast and eclectic	*Bolsters confidence before or during Analogies or Sentence Completions*
I work smart and guess smart	*Reminds you that you are in control, even on the hardest questions*
I am in my SAT groove *or* I'm making each checkpoint *or* My pace is fine	*Restores confidence during a section; good in response to pressure from time constraints*
I am doing my best *or* I will score my best	*Good if you're feeling overwhelmed by a section*
That section is done and I rocked. Bring on the next one *or* I'm ready for the next section	*Transitions you from one section to the next*

Not Just by Saying It

An affirmation will only work on the spot if it means something to you. To make an affirmation meaningful, spend a little time creating it. You may respond best to funny and silly affirmations; then again, you may prefer ones that are soothing and calming. Use the Affirmations on the Spot worksheet to help you develop some statements that can change your mood on the spot.

Affirmations on the Spot Worksheet

I need a confidence boost for these aspects of the SAT:

What are things that I do well on the SAT?

Which of these statements can I use as affirmations on the spot? When might each help me on the test?

Say one of the potential affirmations. How do I feel when I say this affirmation? Focus on those positive feelings for 30 seconds or so. Is this a good affirmation to use? Repeat with the other potential affirmations.

I will use the following affirmations on the spot:

During the weeks that lead up to the test, wake up each morning and say one or more of your affirmations: "I am the SAT Queen." Spend about a minute repeating your affirmation and feeling good about yourself. After you do this a few times, you should notice that simply saying the affirmation makes you feel good.

Gag Me

If this is all a little too touchy-feely for you, try making up statements that are a bit more sarcastic or amusing: "I don't know what I would do with myself if I didn't have the SAT to study for," or, "At least I'm smarter than Jane." Use these statements to laugh about the test and give yourself control over this ridiculous exam. You can also use them to break tension during the test itself.

Try It Out

If you end up in an anxiety-producing situation in the weeks before the SAT, try using an affirmation on the spot. See if it helps you remain calm, or if you need to find a better one. Also, use your affirmation a few times as you do timed SAT sections. The more you use your affirmations, particularly when you're practicing for the SAT, the faster they will calm you during the real test.

Don't Take It Too Seriously

Have you ever played this game?

1. Each player is given a bunch of questions. One person is appointed the timer. No one is to look at the questions before the timer says go.
2. The goal of the game is to get as many questions right as you can within a limited amount of time.
3. When the timer says go, each player attempts to answer correctly as many questions as possible before time runs out. Players can skip questions and return to them later if they have time left.
4. The game has seven rounds. At the end of the seventh round, every player adds up the number of questions she got right. High score wins.

What's the name of the game? The SAT, of course. Did you ever notice how much SAT directions resemble game directions? If more test takers thought of the SAT as a game, there wouldn't be so much test anxiety. Try thinking of the SAT as a game while you practice. See how many questions you can get right in a five-minute period, or how well you can guess smart on a single set of critical reading questions. If you have a study partner, play some games with her, too: Whoever gets the most analogies right on this set doesn't have to pay for the pizza. If you can take the SAT a little less seriously, then you have a better chance of being just a little nervous on test day.

SAT Games

Vocabulary Charades—This is best played with a group of friends. Divide into two teams. Write about ten SAT words per player on slips of paper, and then fold the papers over and place them in a basket. Each player gets one minute to try to get her teammates to guess as many SAT words as possible. When the timer say go, pull a slip of paper from the basket, then try to get your teammates to guess the word by telling them the definition, synonyms, etc. You can't use the word itself, and no skipping words. Teams get one point for each word they guess. Play goes back and forth between the two teams until the words run out.

Math Challenger—Begin by attempting a medium-level math problem from *10 Real SATs* or *Cracking the SAT.* If you get it right, try a hard problem; if you get it wrong, try an easy problem. Every time you get a problem right, jump up to a harder problem. Every time you get a problem wrong, jump down to an easier problem. Give yourself one point for each easy question you get right, two points for each medium question you get right, and three points for each hard question you get right. You can play this game with a study partner, too. Take turns selecting the problems for each other.

Work Smarter—For two or more players. Select a set of quant comp problems and set a time limit. When time begins, each player attempts to solve the problems by working smart—only doing as much work as necessary to get to the answer. When time is called, trade sets. Check your partner's work, giving her one point for a right answer and one point for working smart. If she got an answer right but didn't work smart, show her where she overworked.

Guess Smarter—Also for two or more players. Select a set of critical reading questions and set a time limit. When time begins, each player attempts to smart guess the answers to the questions without reading the passage. When time is called, check your answers against each other without checking the answer key. Work together to determine which answer choices should have been eliminated. Each player gets one point for each time she guessed smart (even if she didn't guess the right answer). If you wish to turn this game into a drill, try this: When you've finished guessing, have each player take out a different-colored pen and work the critical reading passage and questions as you normally would. See how many of your answers stay the same and how many change. How often did you guess the right answer?

TEN-SECOND TENSION BREAKERS

The SAT can make the calmest among us a little tense. It may help to prepare yourself with some quick tension relievers to use on test day if you begin to feel your blood pressure rise. Here are some ten-second tension breakers to use if you get a little tense in the middle of section one, two, three...

Laugh. Just a little, and not loud enough to disturb anyone. Laughing at something—some stupid question on the test, for example—will immediately reduce your tension level. A quick laugh can help you regain your perspective.

Curse. If you're getting really flustered and resenting every second of the section you're on, let it out. While I don't recommend you say your choice words out loud, you can certainly curse that test up one side of the page and down the other with your pencil. Given that no one's going to read your test book, who cares? A few choice words just might be all it takes for you to feel back in control of the test.

Breathe. Don't laugh, but it's important to remember to breathe during the SAT. If you're all tensed up during a section—your shoulders and neck are tight, your breaths short and shallow—stop and take a deep breath. As you do, sit up, stretch out your neck and spine, and let your shoulders relax. Then slowly breathe out through your mouth, imagining that your tension is leaving as you exhale.

SOME FINAL THOUGHTS

Getting nervous is a normal reaction to something stressful. Luckily, you can learn to channel your nervous energy so that you get psyched, instead of stressed, about the SAT. Some people don't find the SAT stressful—good for them. But if you're not one of those people, you don't need to worry. Practice getting psyched for the SAT, create some affirmations to use on the spot, and be ready with some ten-second tension breakers. By the time you take the SAT, you'll be a little nervous—or maybe you won't be nervous at all.

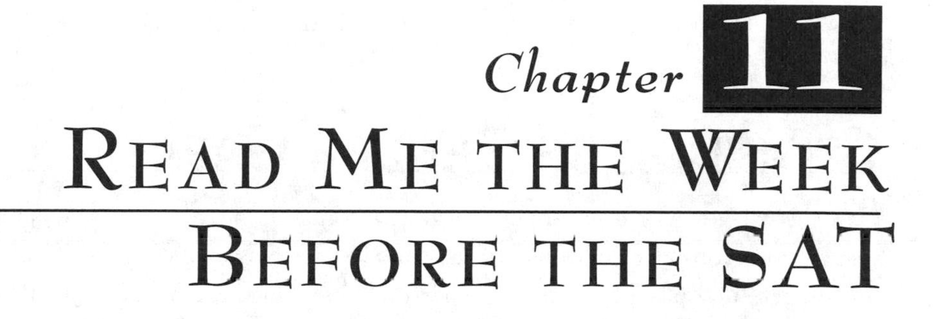

Chapter 11

Read Me the Week Before the SAT

Read Me the Week Before the SAT

The day you've been preparing for is almost here. You've done a lot of work, and although you may feel you still have some final pieces to fit into place, by and large you are prepared. I created this last chapter to make sure you would have everything you need for test day. Take a minute to read through it now. There is a checklist of what you need to bring, some get-psyched and stay-focused exercises for the morning of the test, a bunch of quick reviews, and some warm-up problems. Decide this week which of these you want to do the morning of the SAT.

Closing the Gender Gap?

Can the work you've done these past weeks single-handedly close the gender gap? No, but you'll score your personal best because of it. If you score your personal best on the SAT, and your study partner scores her personal best on the SAT, and your female classmates score their personal best on the SAT, and the female juniors and seniors across the country score their personal best on the SAT, then the gender gap will be a thing of the past. Can you imagine the headline?

Girls Score Higher Than Boys on the SAT for the First Time in History

ETS and the College Board announced today that, for the first time in history, girls outscored boys on the SAT by a margin of...

You go, girl! I'll be checking the headlines.

Day of the Test

Where are you taking the test? ______________________________

Do you have or need directions? ______________________________

What time do you need to be there? ______________________________

What time do you need to get up? ______________________________

Day of Test Checklist

- ☐ Registration confirmation
- ☐ Picture I.D.
- ☐ Two or more sharpened no.2 pencils with good erasers
- ☐ Watch
- ☐ Calculator
- ☐ An inconspicuous snack
- ☐ Water
- ☐ Sweater/Sweatshirt
- ☐ Tissues (if you need them)
- ☐ Any other personal items (if you need them)

Concentration Techniques and Stress Reducers I Plan to Use

Before the morning of the SAT, write down the concentration techniques and the stress reducers that you plan to use during the test.

GET-PSYCHED EXERCISE

Do this one more time, the morning of the test.

At my best in the past . . .

Describe one or two situations in which you were at your best—feeling on top of the world, invincible, excellent

Focus on the feelings you had. Write down some words or phrases to describe how you felt at the time. Example: *I felt in control, I was confident*

At my best today . . .

Now use those phrases to describe yourself in the present tense: *I am in control, I am confident*

Use your affirmations to describe yourself in relation to the SAT: *I am in control of the SAT, I feel secure about the SAT*

My Personal Testing Space

To be done as soon as you're seated for the SAT.

Once you're seated, outline your personal testing space with your arms. Sit in this position as you stare down at your desk (or table) for a minute or so.

- Remove your arms from the space.
- Imagine that your testing boundaries are still in place.
- Focus yourself within this space.

If you become distracted during the test, sit up straight and briefly recreate your boundaries with your arms. Refocus yourself, and then continue working.

MY MATH STRATEGY

Section	I will do_____questions; my checkpoint is_____minutes					
	Easy		Medium		Hard	
	#	Minutes	#	Minutes	#	Minutes
30 Minutes 25 Reg Math	All					
15 Minutes 10 Reg Math	All					

	Quant Comp				Grid-In			
	Easy	Med	Hard	Minutes	Easy	Med	Hard	Minutes
30 Minutes 15 Quant Comp 10 Grid-In	All				All			

My Verbal Strategy

Section	I will do____questions; my checkpoint is____minutes					
	Sentence Comp		Analogies		Critical Reading	
	#	Minutes	#	Minutes	#	Minutes
30 Minutes 9 Sentence Comp 6 Analogies 15 Critical Reading						
30 Minutes 10 Sentence Comp 13 Analogies 12 Critical Reading						
15 Minutes 13 Critical Reading						

Works Cited

American Association of University Women (AAUW). Shortchanging Girls, Shortchanging America: Executive Summary. Washington, D.C.: American Association of University Women, 1994.

American Association of University Women (AAUW) Gender Gaps: Where Schools Still Fail Our Children. Washington, D.C.: American Association of University Women Educational Foundation, 1998.

Benfer, Amy. "Lost Boys." Salon, 5 February 2002. <www.salon.com>.

Blooston, George. "SATs and the Battle of the Sexes." Smart Talk: News, Views & Attitudes. Savvy Woman. April 1989: 17–18.

Cole, Nancy S. The ETS Gender Study: How Females and Males Perform in Educational Settings. Princeton, New Jersey: Educational Testing Service, 1997.

Coley, Richard. Differences in the Gender Gap: Comparisons Across Racial/Ethnic Groups in Education and Work. Princeton, New Jersey: Educational Testing Service, 2001.

College Entrance Examination Board (College Board). "The New SAT: Press Releases." College Board Online, 27 June 2002. <http://www.collegeboard.com/about/newsat/press.html>.

College Entrance Examination Board (College Board). "The New SAT: Fairness." College Board Online, 27 June 2002. <http://www.collegeboard.com/about/newsat/satfaqs/fairness.html>.

College Entrance Examination Board (College Board). "Percentile Ranks for Males, Females, and Total Group: 2001 College Bound Seniors." College Board Online. <www.collegeboard.com>.

College Entrance Examination Board (College Board). "Research Summary SAT and Gender Differences." RS-04 February (1998).

College Entrance Examination Board (College Board). "SAT I: Reasoning Test."

College Board Online, 14 June 2002. <www.collegeboard.com/sat/html/admissions/about001.html>.

College Entrance Examination Board (College Board). *10 Real SATs*. New York: College Entrance Examination Board, 2000.

College Entrance Examination Board (College Board). "What Should You Know About the SAT I: Reasoning Test?" Career Explorer, 2 July 2002. <http://www.careerexplorer.net/articles/sat.asp>.

Dean, Cathy. "Traumatic Tests: Gender Bias and the SATs." 10 May 1997. <http://home.earthlink.net/~ifdean/sat.html>

Educational Testing Service. Overview: ETS Fairness Review. Princeton, New Jersey: Educational Testing Service, 2002.

FairTest. "FairTest: University Testing/2001 SAT Scores." 26 April 2002. <www.fairtest.org>.

FairTest. "Gender Bias in College Admissions Tests." 26 April 2002. <www.fairtest.org>.

FairTest. "Gender Bias in NCAA Eligibility Requirements." 26 April 2002. <www.fairtest.org>.

FairTest. "Questions for College Board Trustees About Proposed Revisions to the SAT I." 11 July 2002. <www.fairtest.org>.

FairTest. "The SAT: Questions and Answers." 5 April 2001. <www.fairtest.org>.

FairTest. "SAT Repacking Fails to Address Fundamental Flaws, May Increase Exam's Bias and Coachability; FairTest and Allies Urge More Colleges to Drop Test Score Requirements, Stop SAT Misuse." FairTest Press Release, 11 July 2002. <www.fairtest.org>.

FairTest. "SAT Scores Not Needed For Fair, Valid College Admissions." FairTest Press Release, 28 August 2001. <www.fairtest.org>.

FairTest. "2000 College Bound Seniors Test Scores: SAT." 26 April 2002. <www.fairtest.org>.

Gipps, Caroline, and Patricia Murphy. *A Fair Test? Assessment, Achievement and Equity.* Philadelphia: Open University Press, 1994.

Gurian, Michael. *Boys and Girls Learn Differently: A Guide for Teachers and Parents.* 2001. San Francisco: Jossey-Bass, 2002.

Hood, Albert B., and Richard W. Johnson. "Ethical and Social Issues in Testing—Part 2." Assessment in Counseling: A Guide to the Use of Psychological Assessment Procedures, Second Edition (1998). ACAeNews: 2 July 2002. <www.counseling.org/enews/volume_1/0108c.htm>.

Kafer, Krista. "Wasting Education Dollars: The Women's Educational Equity Act." The Heritage Foundation Backgrounder, 11 October 2001. <www.heritage.org/Research/Education/BG1490.ctm>.

Kessel, Cathy, and Marcia C. Linn. "Grades or Scores: Predicting Future College Mathematics Performance." Educational Measurement: Issues and Practice. Winter 1996: 10–14, 38.

Leonard, David K., and Jiming Jiang. "Gender Bias and the College Predictions of the SATs: A Cry of Despair." Research in Higher Learning 40.4, (1999), 375–407.

Levinson, Arlene. "SAT Scores Similar to Last Year." The Associated Press, 28 August 2001.

Orenstein, Peggy. *Schoolgirls: Young Women, Self-Esteem, and the Confidence Gap.* 1994. New York: Anchor Books, 1995, 2000.

Selkow, Paula. *Assessing Sex Bias in Testing.* Westport, Connecticut: Greenwood Press, 1984.

Willingham, Warren W., and Nancy S. Cole. *Gender and Fair Assessment.* Mahwah, New Jersey: Lawrence Erlbaum Associates, 1997.

Wilson, Trish. "Boys May Not Be Better At Math After All." Chicago Sun-Times, 13 January 2002. <www.suntimes.com/output/education/cst-nws-math13.html>.

About the Author

Alexandra Freer has been teaching students how to beat the SAT since 1987. In her years as Executive Director of The Princeton Review in New Jersey, Alex not only helped prepare thousands of students for the SAT, LSAT, GMAT, GRE and MCAT, but also worked closely with the company's Research & Development staff to refine The Princeton Review's materials and test-taking strategies. Alex's writing credits include *The Grad Pack: Cracking the System for the LSAT CD-ROM*, *Cracking the System for the SAT 2000 Edition*, and *Cracking the AP Psychology Exam*. Alex lives at the beach in New Jersey and is never too busy for a barefoot walk in the sand.

The Princeton Review
Better Scores. Better Schools.

The Princeton Review
Better Scores. Better Schools.